Scot Ranney's Jazz Piano Notebook

jazz piano exercises, etudes, and tricks of the trade you can use today

Volume 2 of Scot Ranney's "Jazz Piano Notebook" series:

"latinesque"

by Scot Ranney

ISBN: 978-1-365-72480-0

First Edition

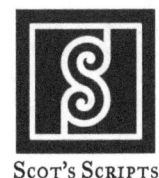

Scot's Scripts

www.scotsscripts.com

TABLE OF CONTENTS

Acknowledgements:

Special thanks to my Mom, Jeff Brent, Tim Richards and everyone else who has helped me keep this book on track and get it out there.

"*A chimpanzee could learn to do what I do physically. But it goes way beyond that. When you play, you play life.*"

~ *Jaco Pastorius*

THE THING ABOUT JAZZ IMPROVISATION

Jazz is art wrapped in science and physical technique.

We practice technique so our art isn't held back by our fingers. We study theory and ear training so we can play the melodies and harmonies we intend to. Art happens when our tools and knowledge come together in a conversation in the language of music.

Technique for pianists is especially important because each key on the piano feels physically different for our hands. Jazz piano studies help your hands grab sounds without losing the moment by thinking about it.

For example, a 5th on a keyboard can feel completely different depending on the key you're in:

- white to white such as the keys of C and F
- black to white such as the key of Bb
- white to black such as the key of B
- black to black such as the keys of Eb and Ab

Scales, arpeggios, patterns, and other exercises help you feel the keyboard which helps your improvisation flow more naturally because your hands and fingers are ready for whatever is coming next.

Technique can not be understated because good technique lets your fingers do anything, in any key, at any speed. Mediocre technique makes everything more difficult, especially on the piano.

How to Use This Book

Play through it as fast as you can without worrying about comprehension. Mark interesting spots with bookmark stickers for later focus. When finished, go back through it thorougly and work on the parts that you really need to.

Book Notes

1. Sometimes I've written notes like F♭ instead of E. In "real life" you wouldn't want to do this because it makes music harder to read, but here I want to write them how they are being used harmonically.

2. Most of the exercises are in 12 keys because 12 key playing is super important, especially when accompanying vocalists.

Fifteen minutes of focusing on something in 12 keys makes everything else easier.

3. This is not a jazz piano method book, it's a book that has musical ideas that I enjoying playing and hopefully you will enjoy playing as well!

Some of the material in this book will be challenging if you're not used to reading music. Start slow and don't practice mistakes. You are invited to ask any questions you might have in the forums at LearnJazzPiano.com.

Videos of the pieces: https://www.youtube.com/user/ScotRanney/playlists

~Scot Ranney

Calypso Exercise 1

A fun exercise based off a calypso jazz piano lick.

This lick can be used as an introduction for a calypso jazz song. Monty Alexander uses something like this as an intro for the song, "Funji Mama" on the album "Triple Treat" with Ray Brown and Herb Ellis. The original "Funji Mama" is by Blue Mitchell and is worth listening to with a young Chic Corea tearing it up on the piano. Slurs are notated in the first key and should be used in the same way throughout the exercise.

Scot Ranney

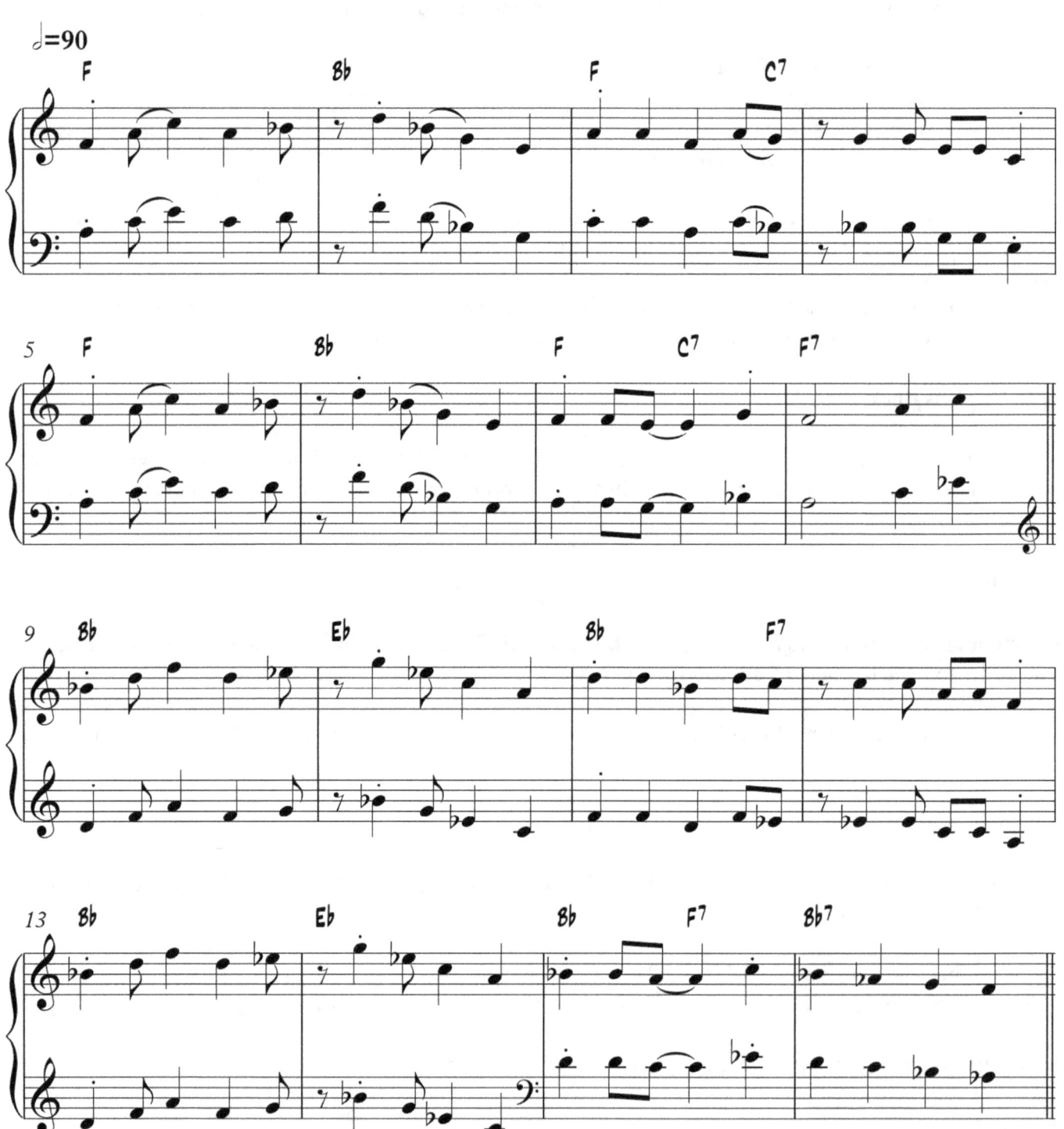

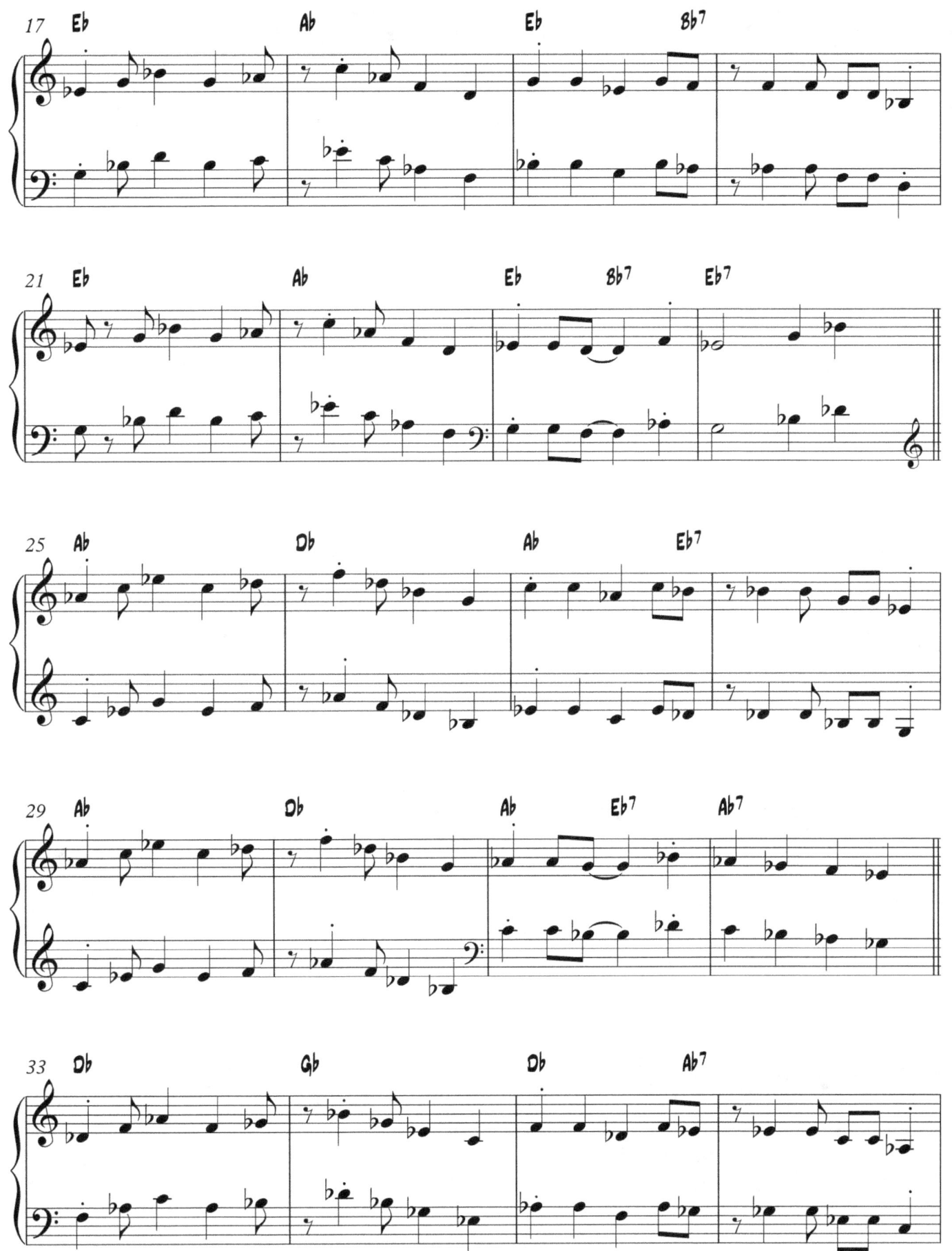

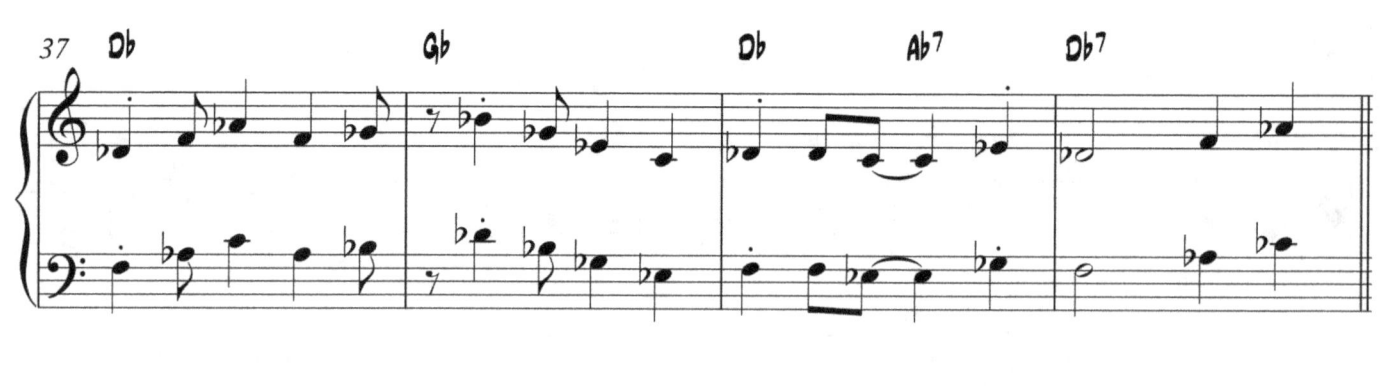

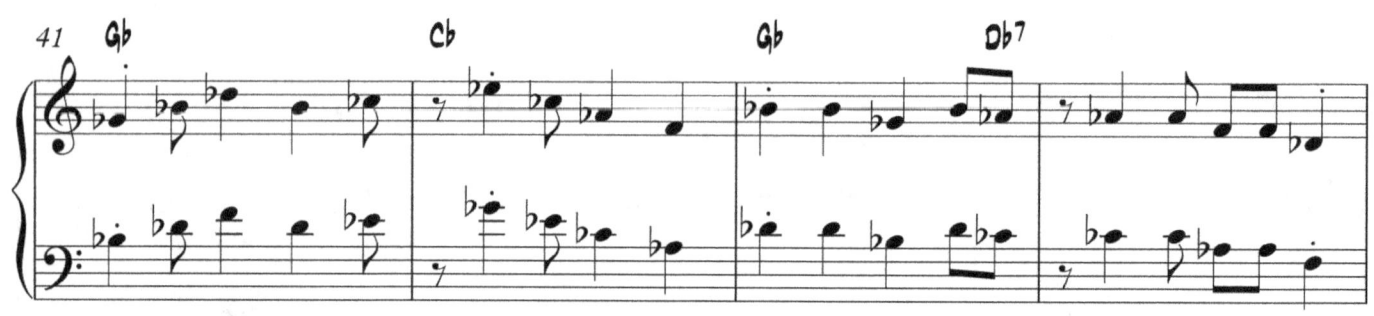

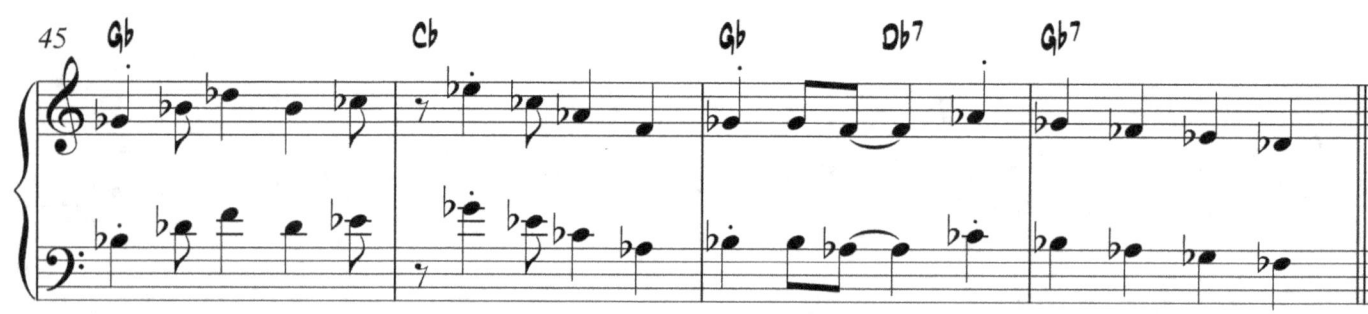

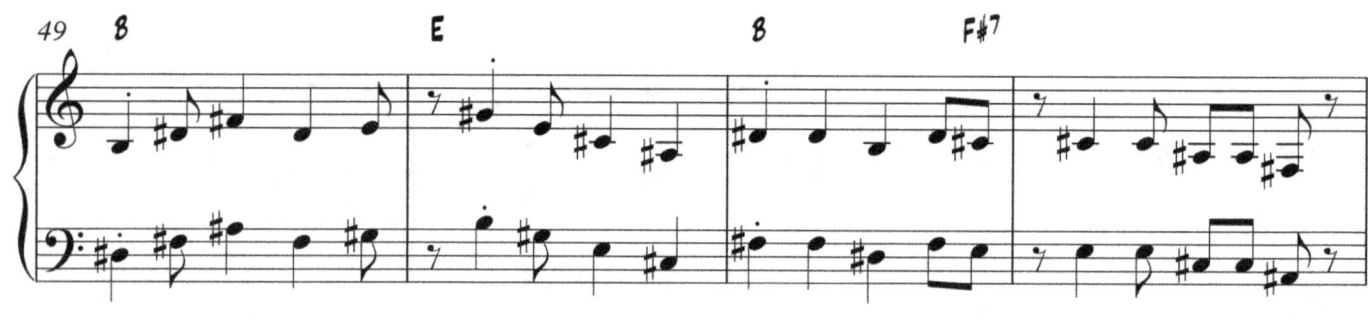

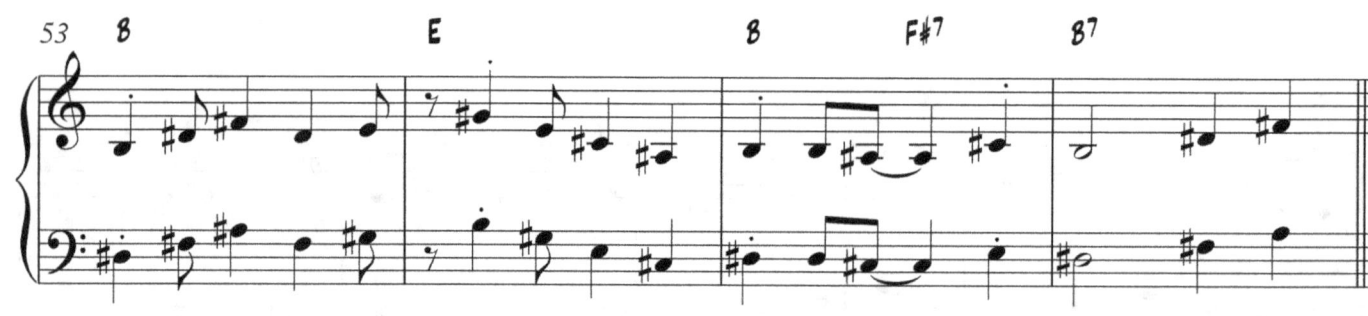

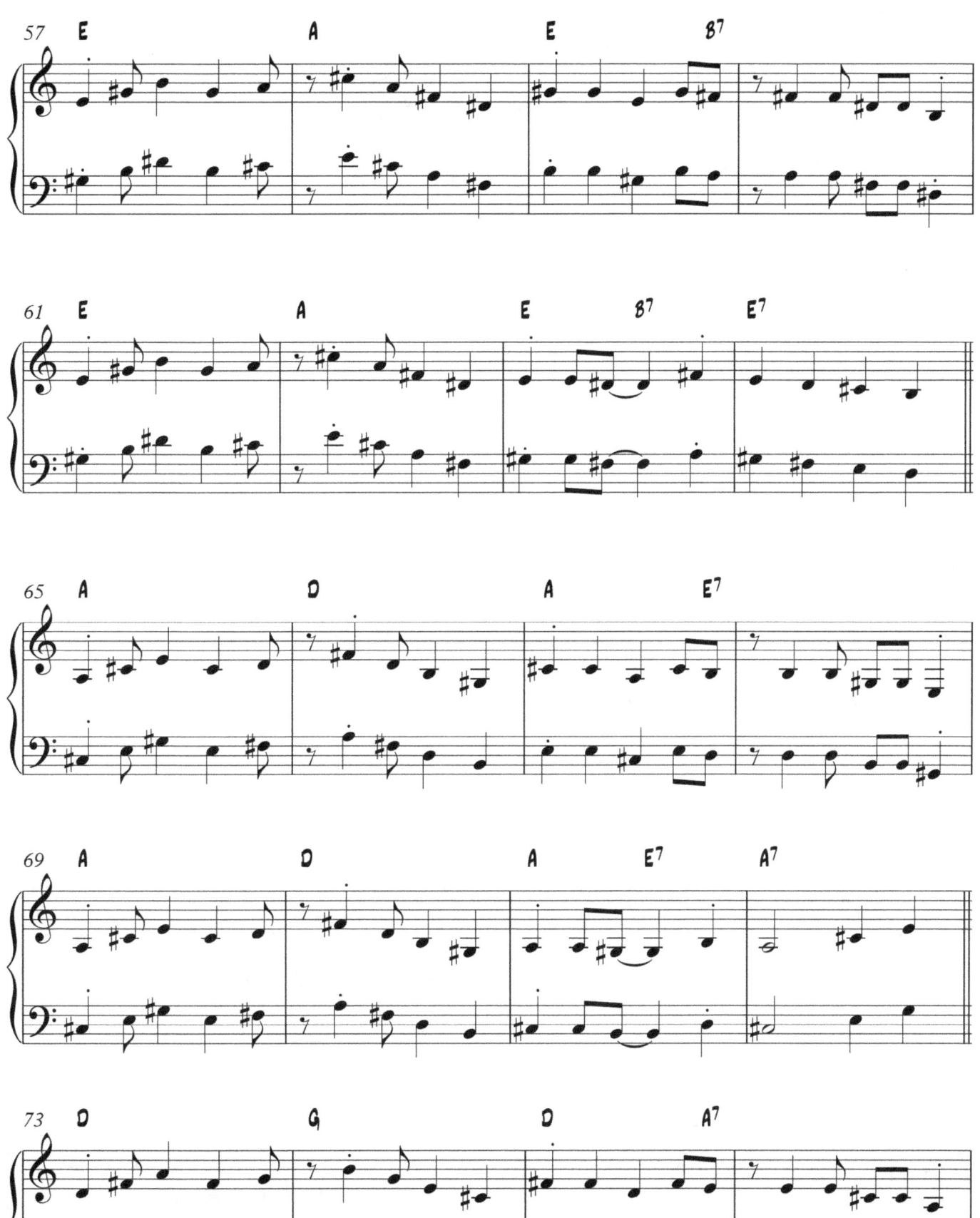

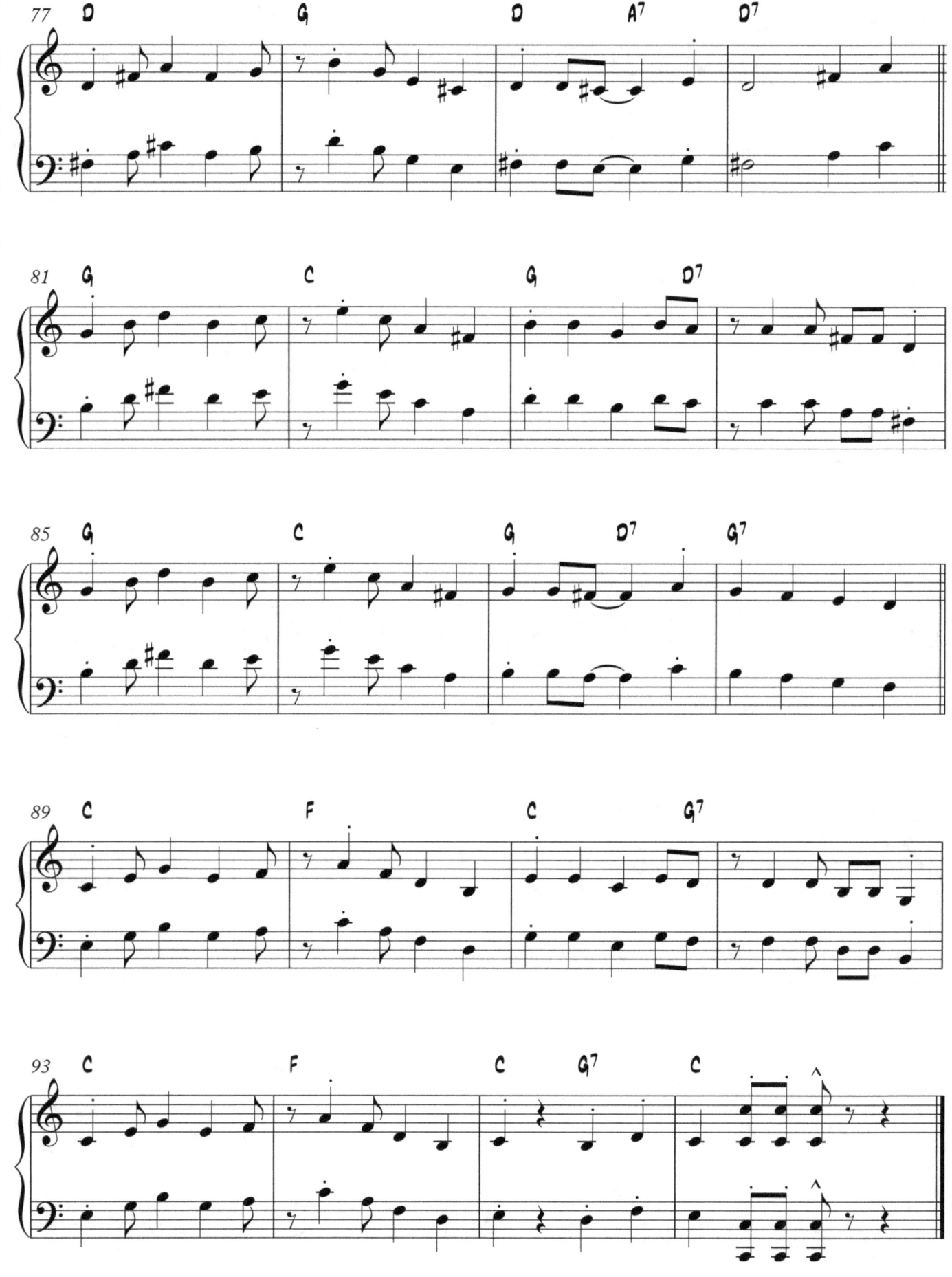

CALYPSO PROGRESSIONS

These progresions groove and can be used to set up the band

Work up the following four progressions in all keys. These are useful in many styles because they are basically rhythm changes with ascending bass lines.

Once you have these grooves under your fingers and can play them without changing tempo, try some variations. Rhythmic variations, melodic alterations, anything is cool as long as you practice the same variation over different keys until you can do it without thinking.

I like to play grooves like this in 12 keys, just the groove until it flows naturally. I don't try improvising on this or any other groove I'm working on until flows naturally. Once it's flowing, I'll start jamming on the bass pattern until I feel comfortable, then I'll try changing the key (and always try harder keys first!) Sometimes I change the key by half steps, other times fourths or fifths, no matter what, I'm always trying to keep things fresh and challenging when I practice.

Scot Ranney

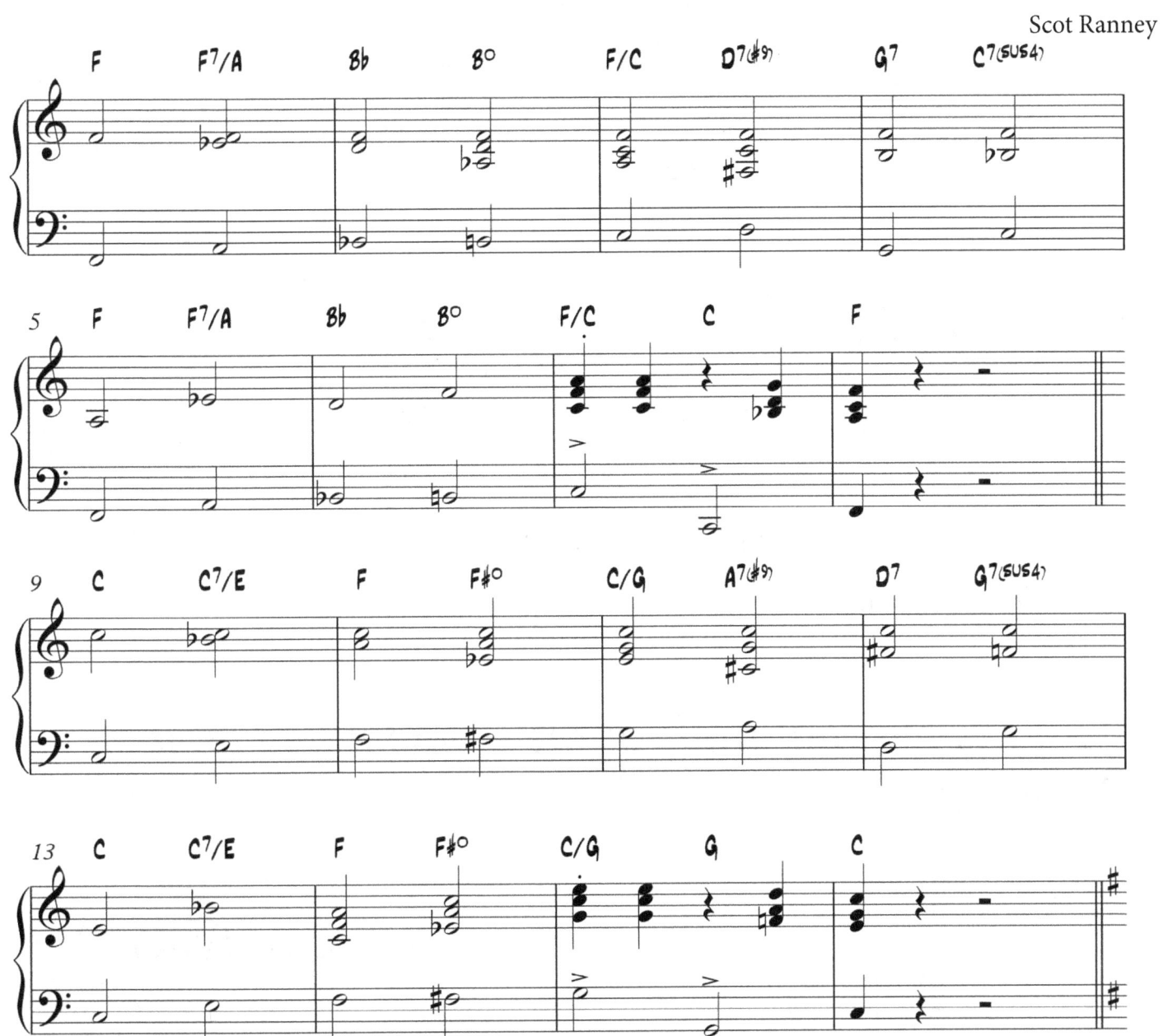

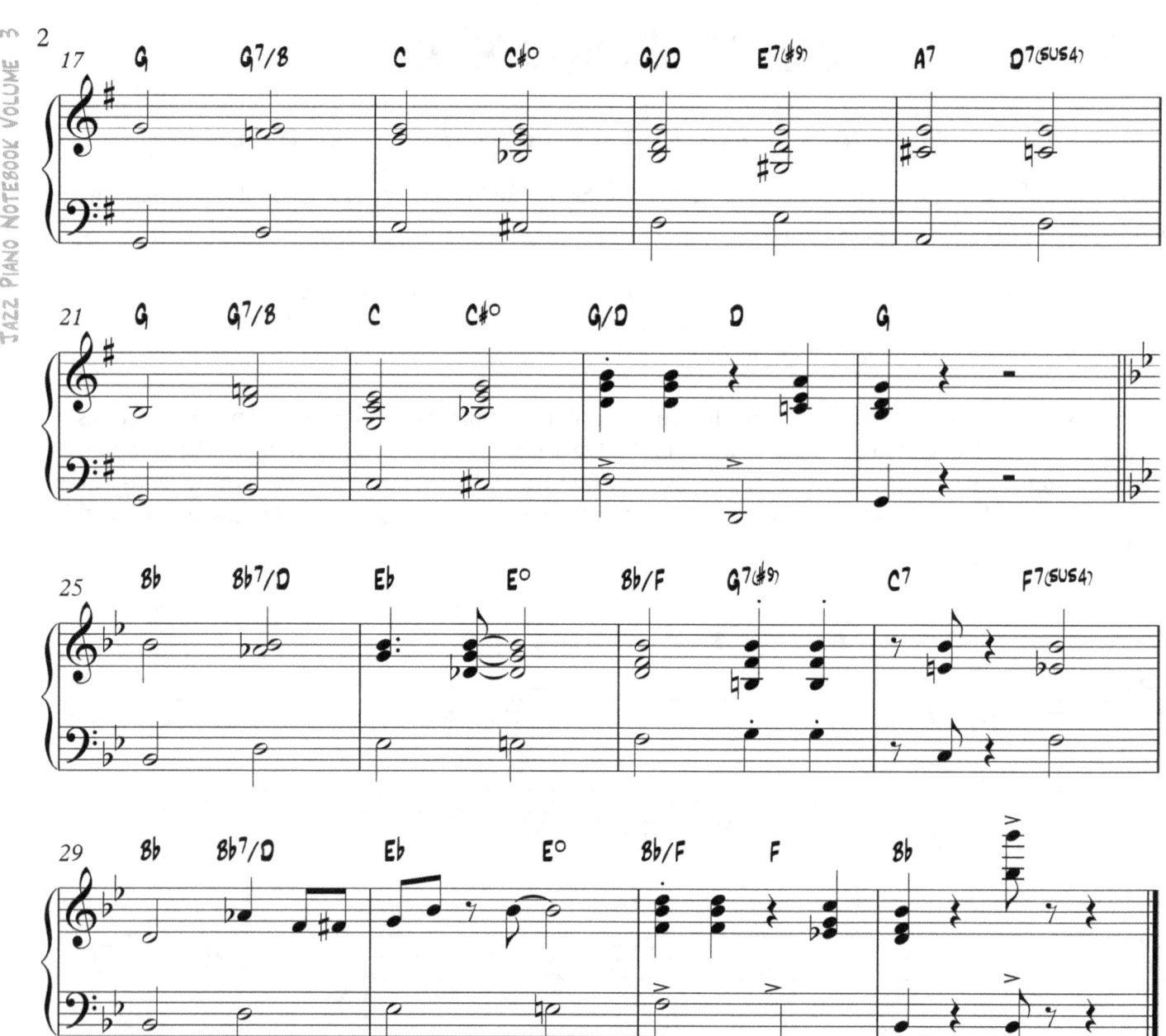

Why practice all this stuff? So you can play what you hear without your fingers getting in the way.

"I try to play naturally at the moment and let it happen."

~McCoy Tyner

Calypso Exercise 2

This exercise is based on buttery goodness.

Sonny Rollins recorded a song called "Brown Skin Girl" and this exercise is based off a lick from that tune. Rollins got this from a Jamaican folk song.

Play this light and rhythmically and at about 120 for the quarter note. It should be a happy sound, reminiscent of steel drums and the beach. Start slow and be precise so you don't practice mistakes.

Scot Ranney

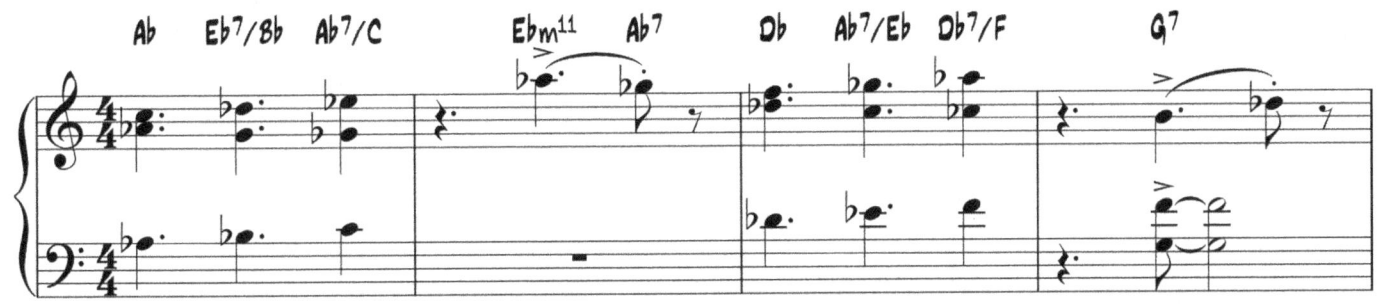

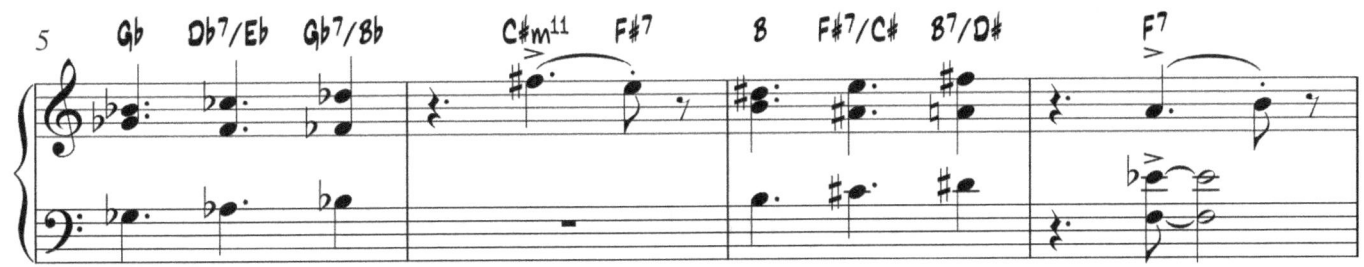

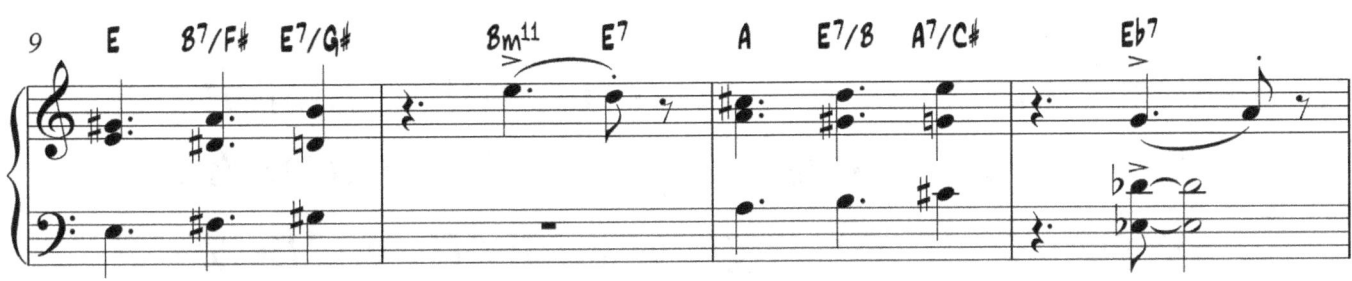

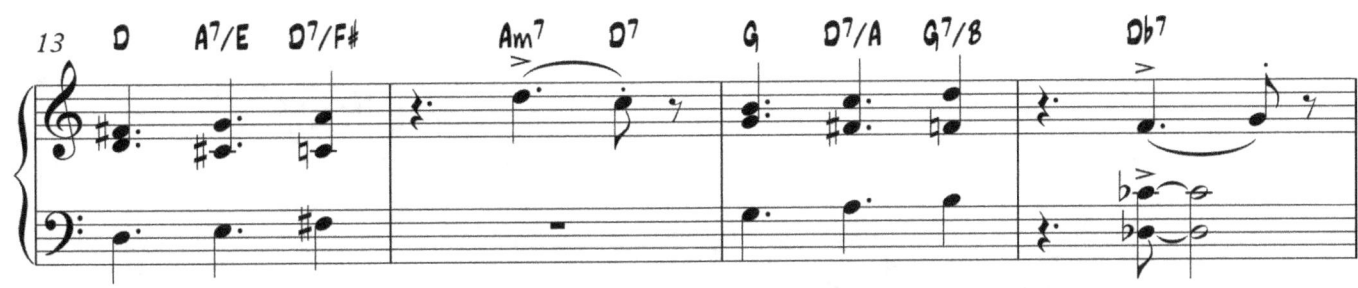

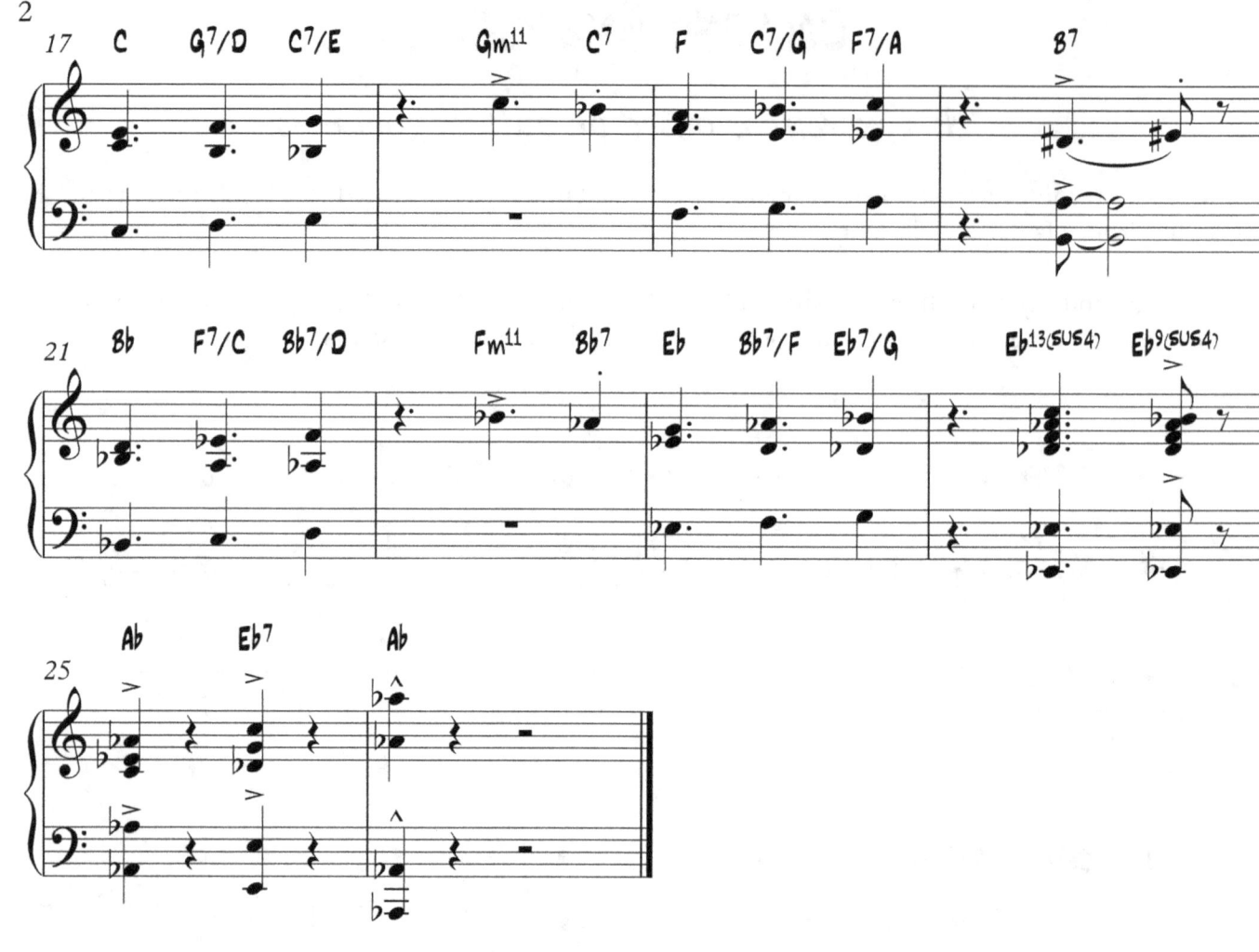

Want to get good? Want to get good fast? Watch and listen to as much live music as you can.

"I got a chance to listen to and watch Thelonious Monk and his quartet play two shows a night, for six weeks. It was a great education. There was my university, man."

~Chick Corea

CHICO'S REVENGE

An Original Calypso Song

This is a tune I play solo piano or with my funkadellic swing reggae band, "Chico's Paradise." Chico is a little lime green red eyed tree frog from a jungle somewhere near the equator. Solo over changes.

Scot Ranney

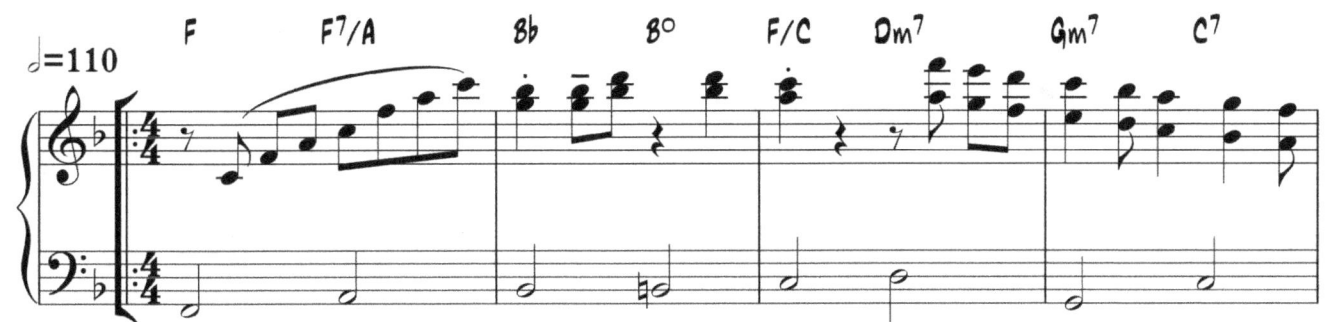

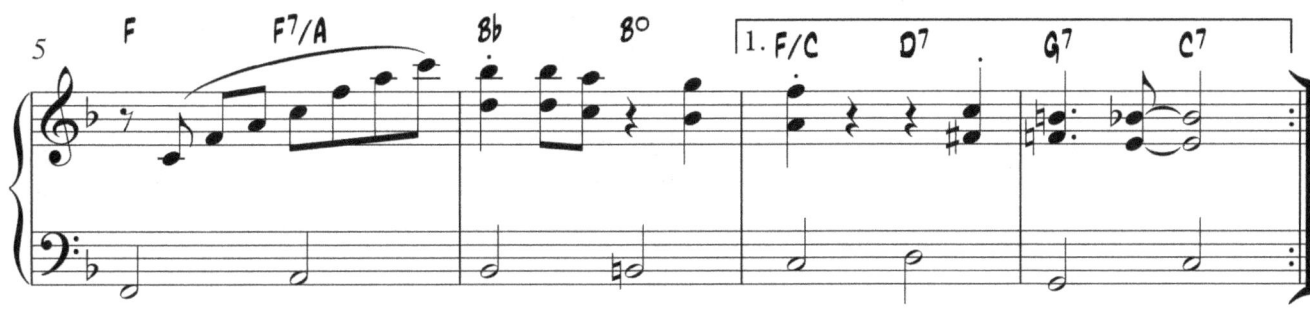

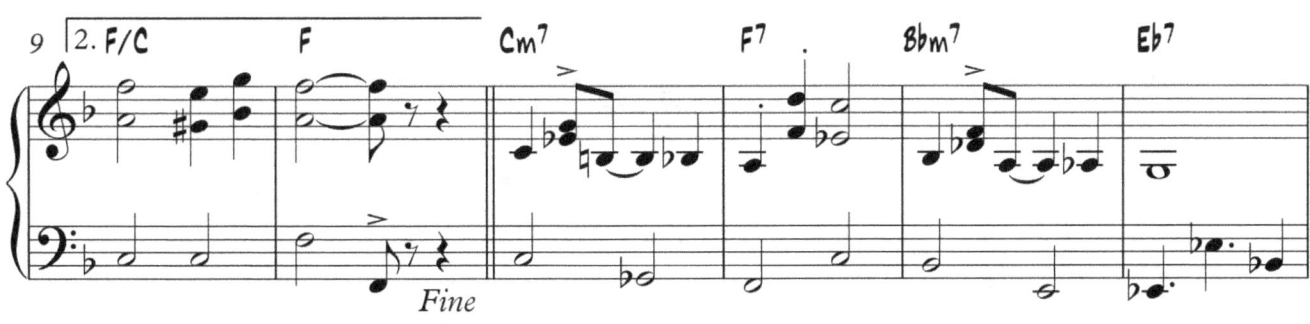

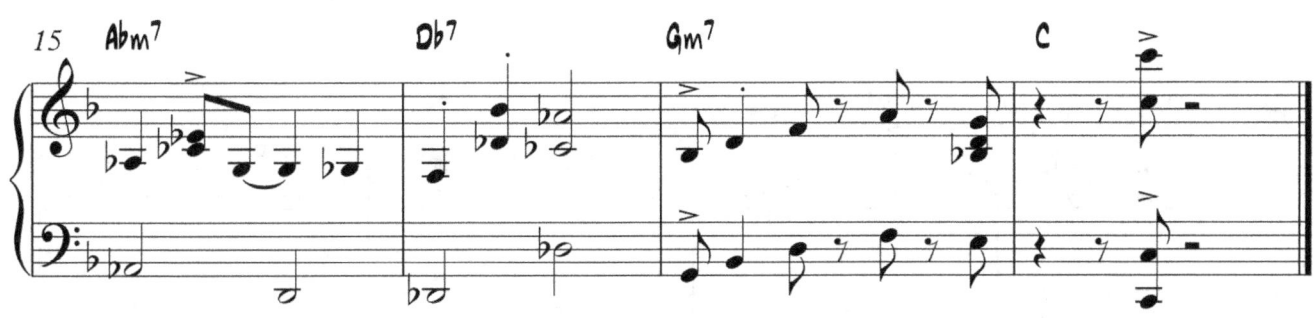

D.C. al Fine - take 2nd ending on DC

Calypso Exercise 3

A good one for your fingers.

This is also based off "Brown Skin Girl" by Sonny Rollins. Emebed this idea into your fingers so it comes out when you're jamming. Check out "St. Thomas," another Sonny Rollins must-know tune.

Scot Ranney

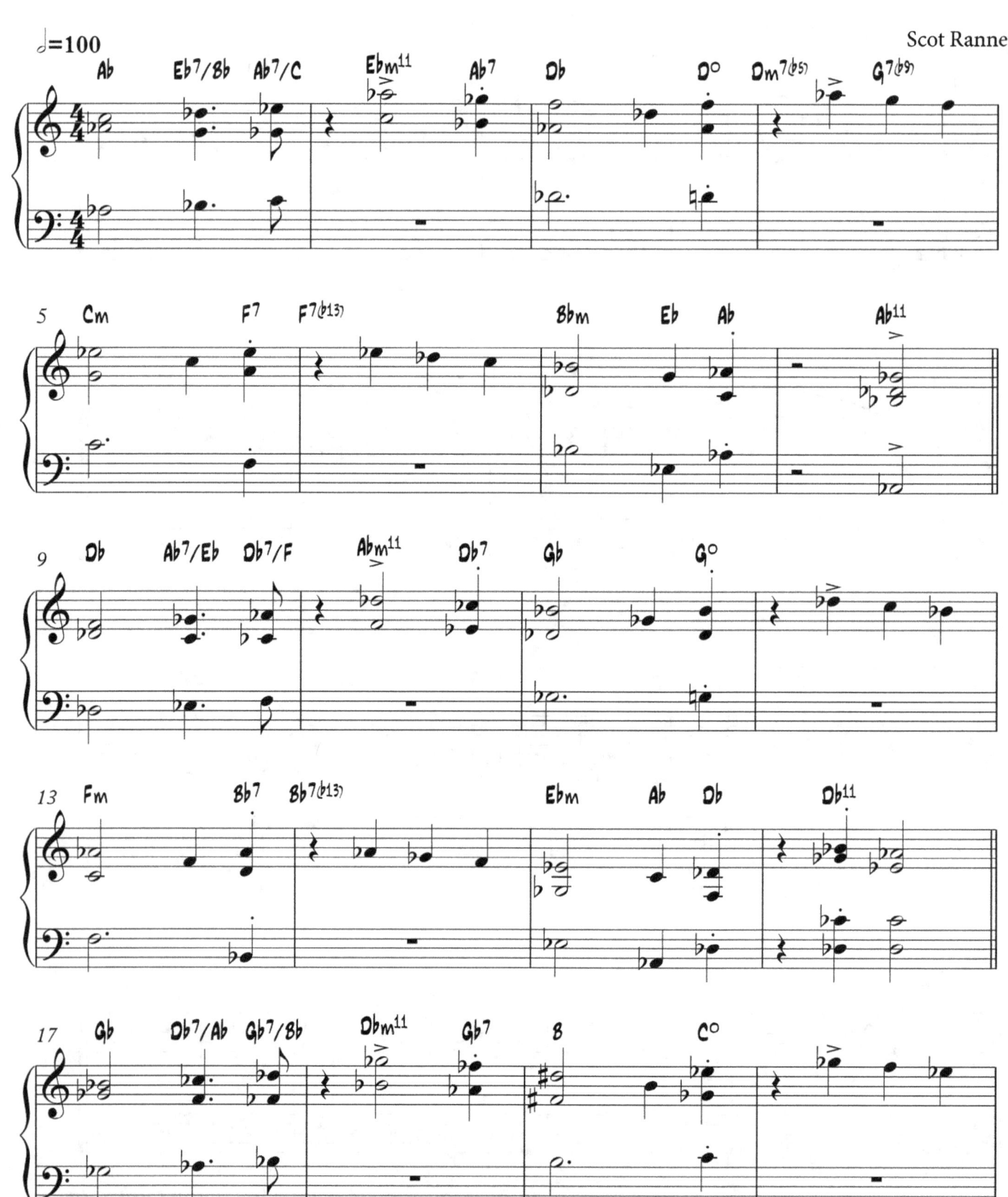

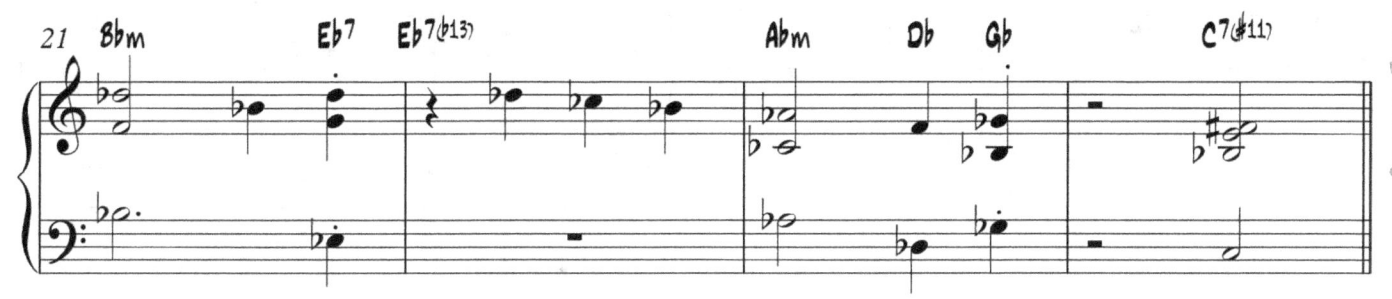

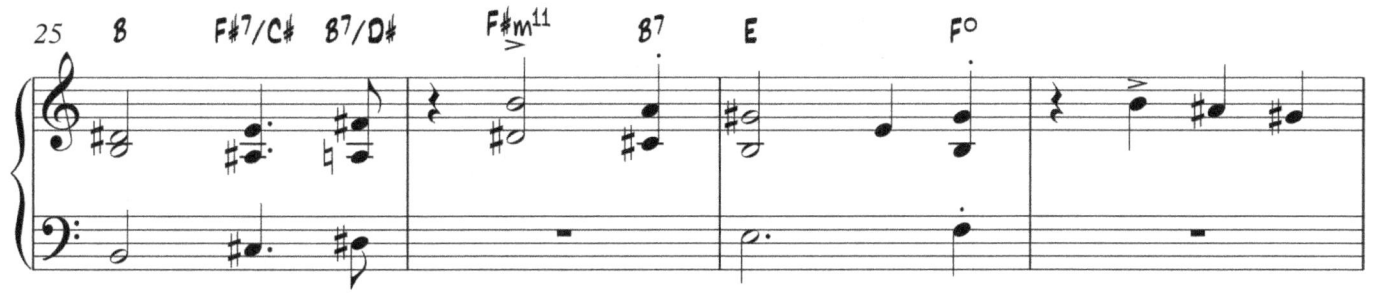

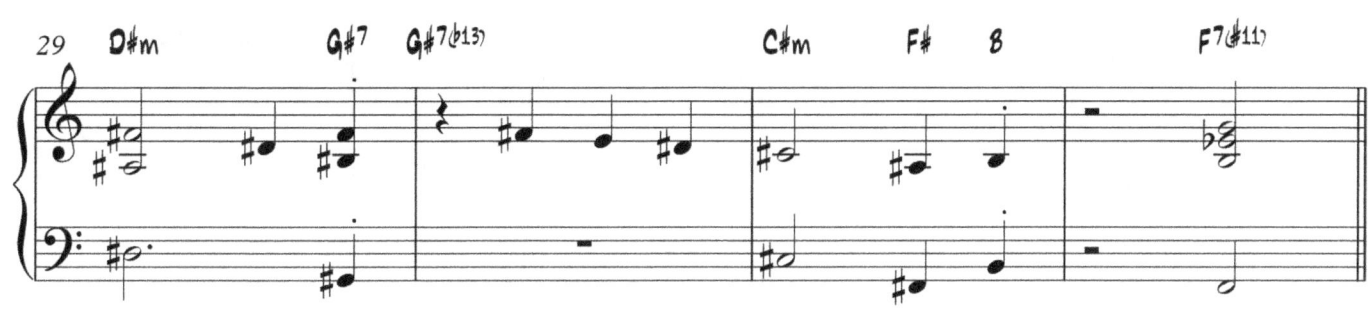

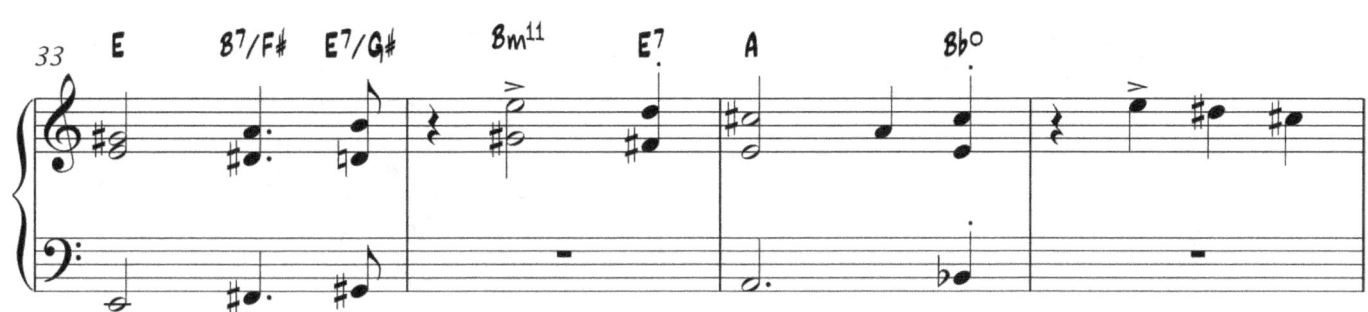

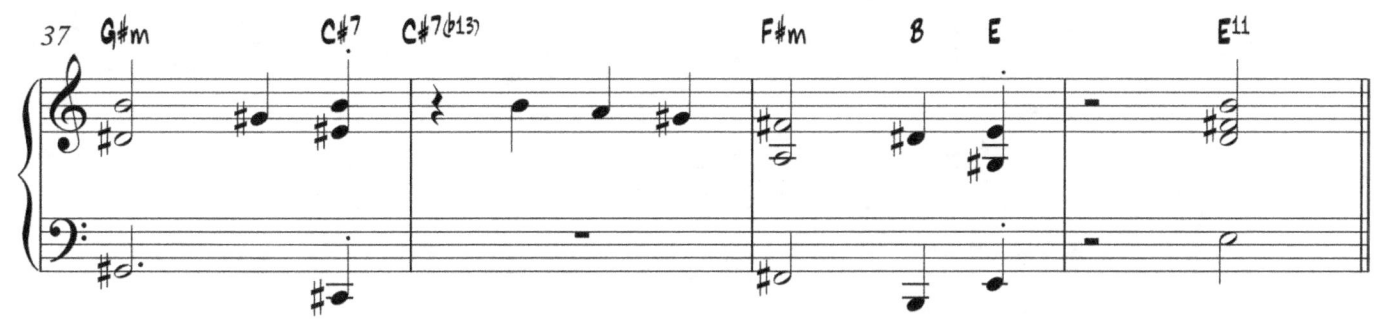

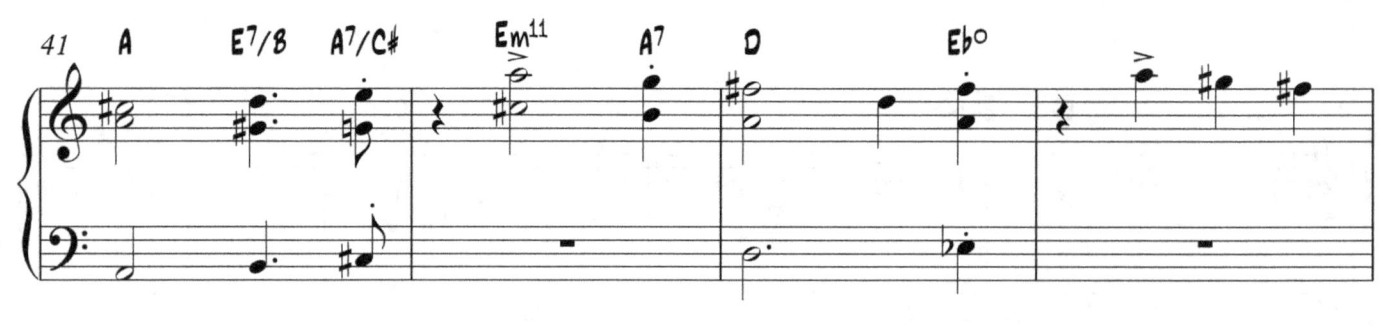

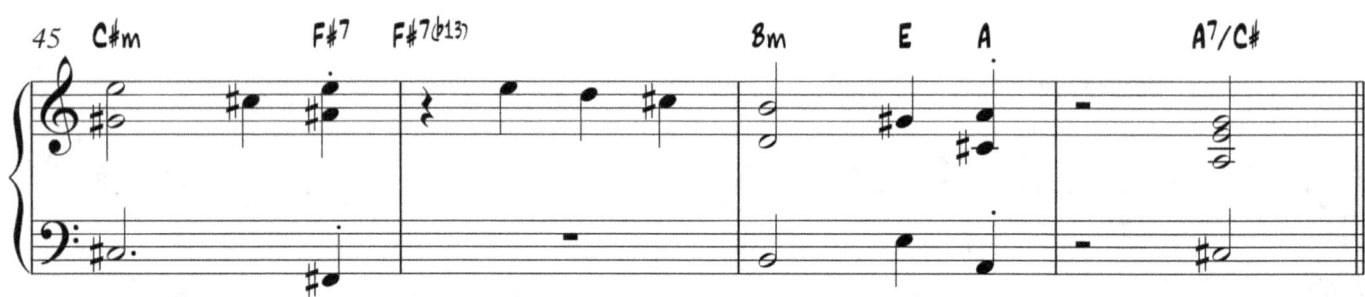

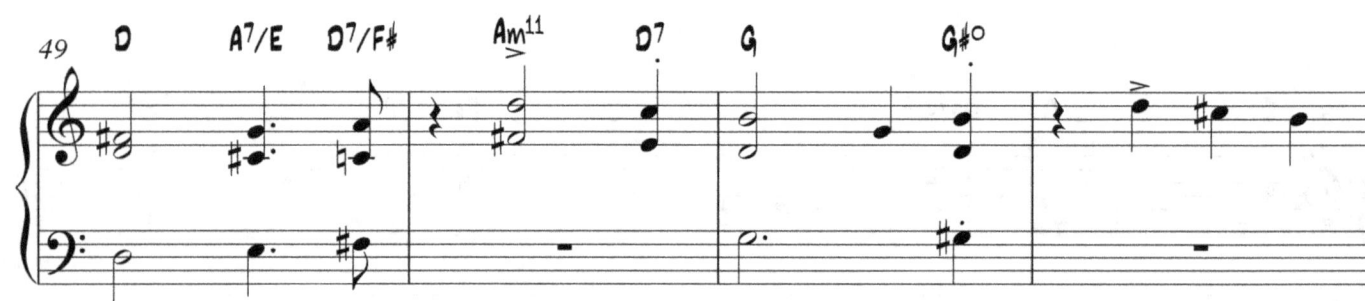

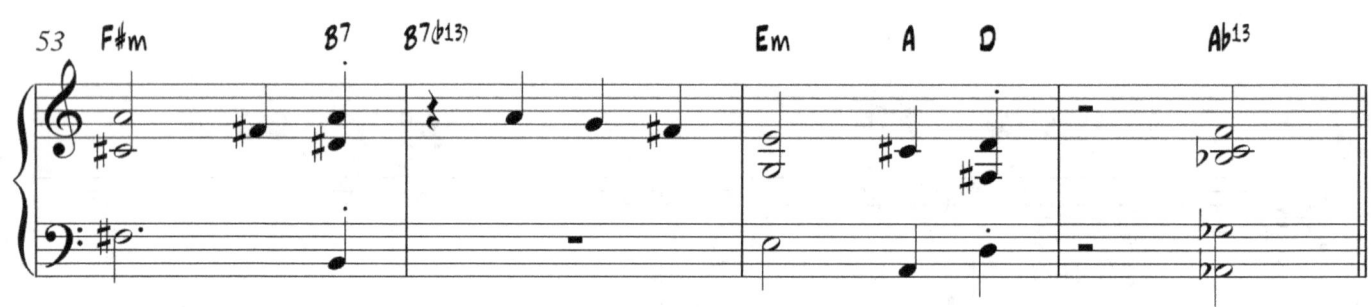

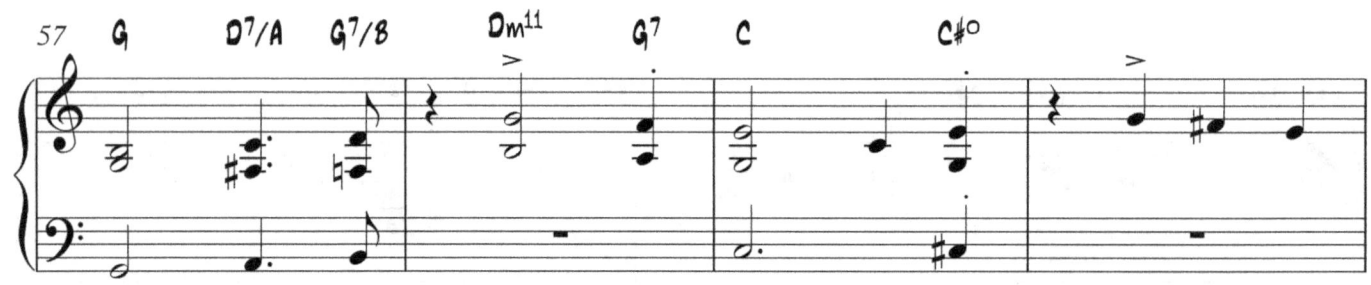

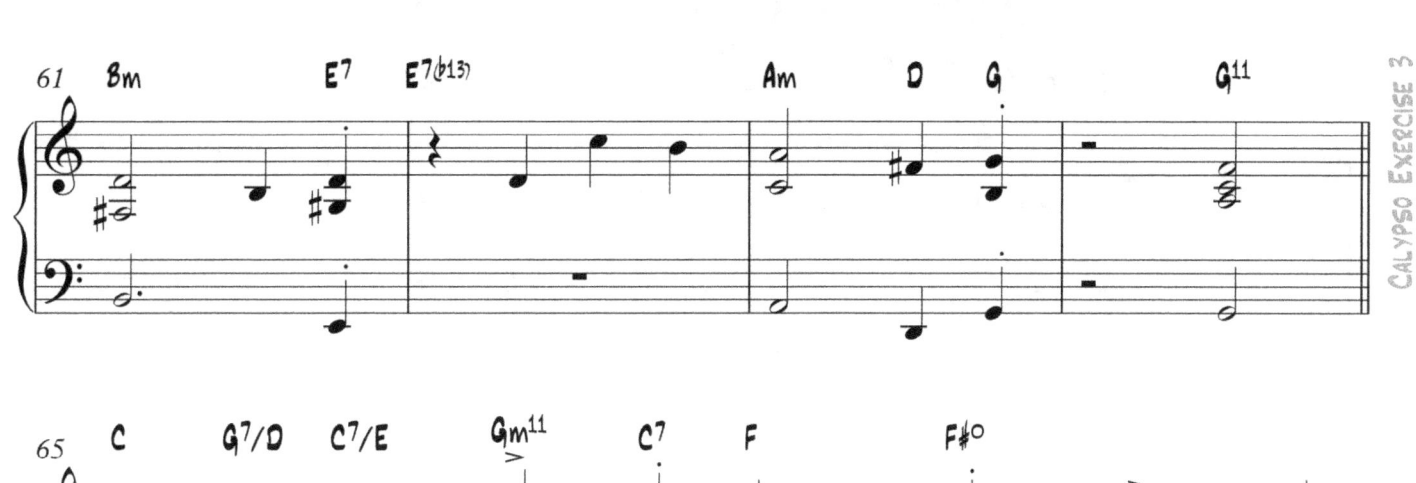

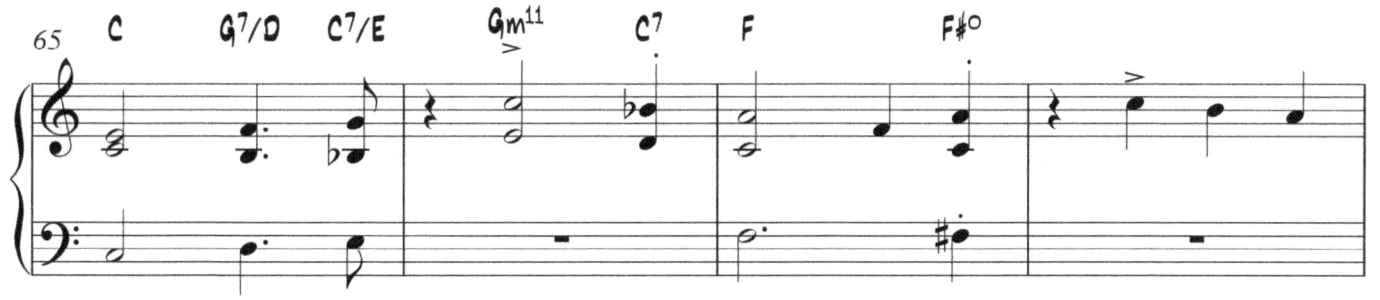

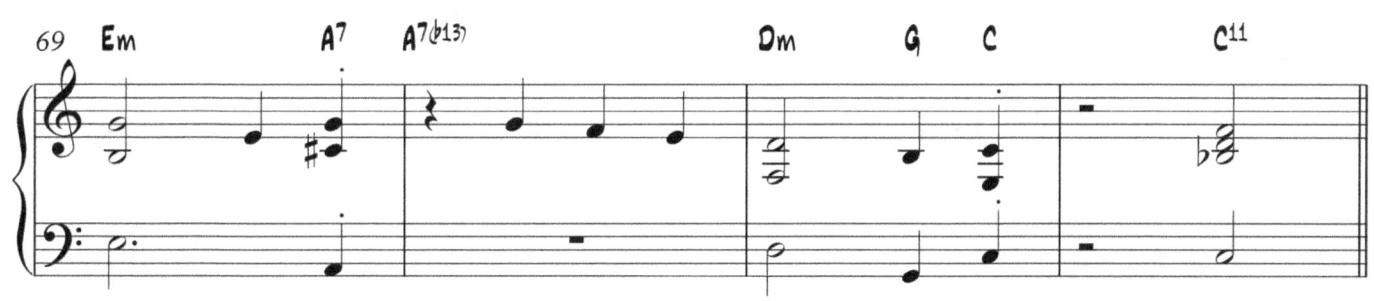

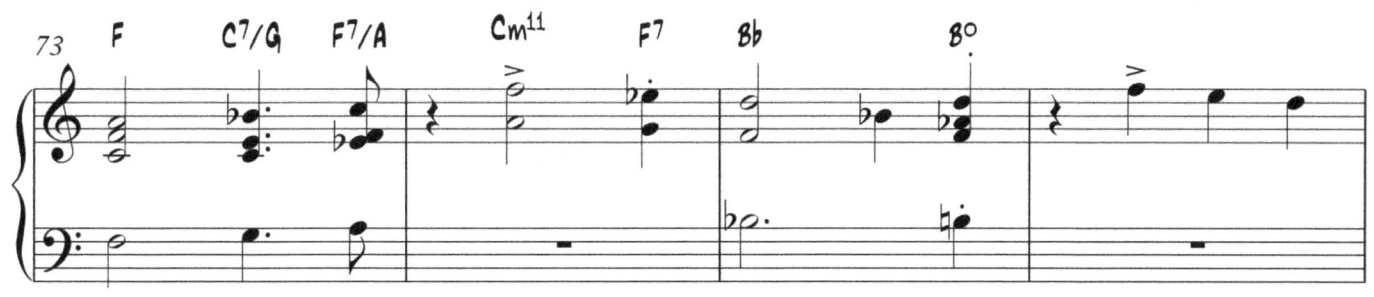

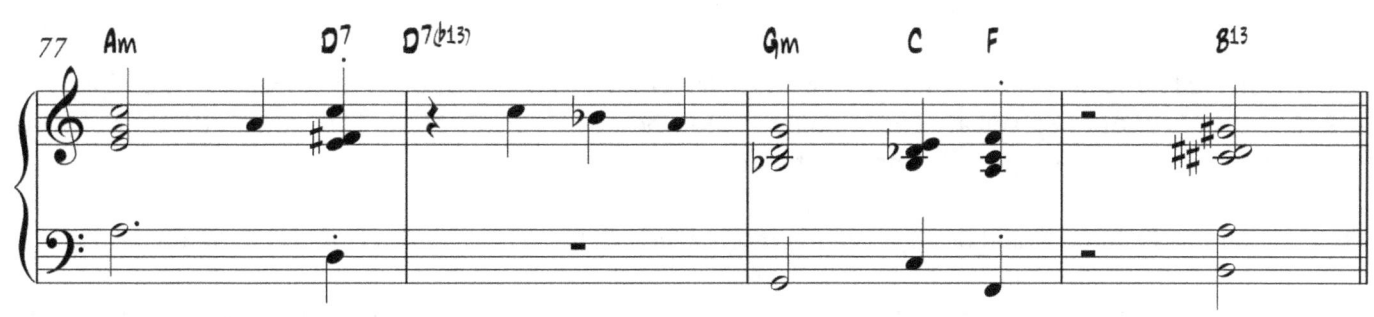

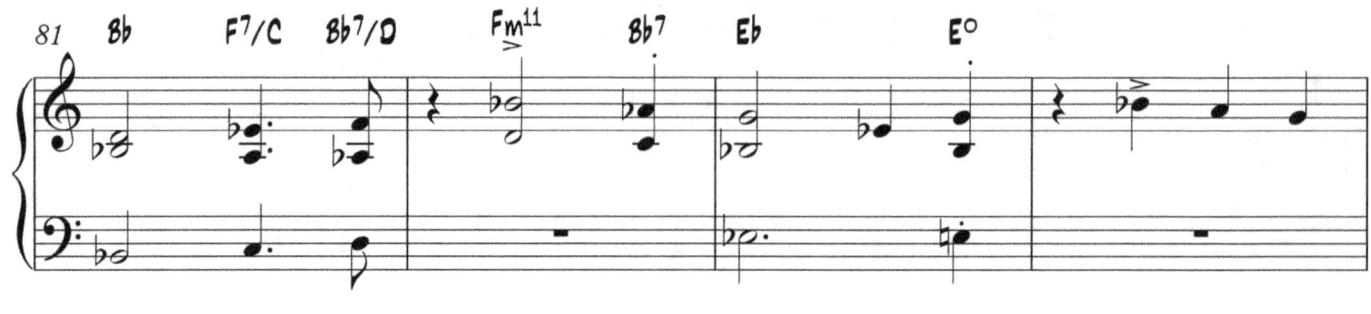

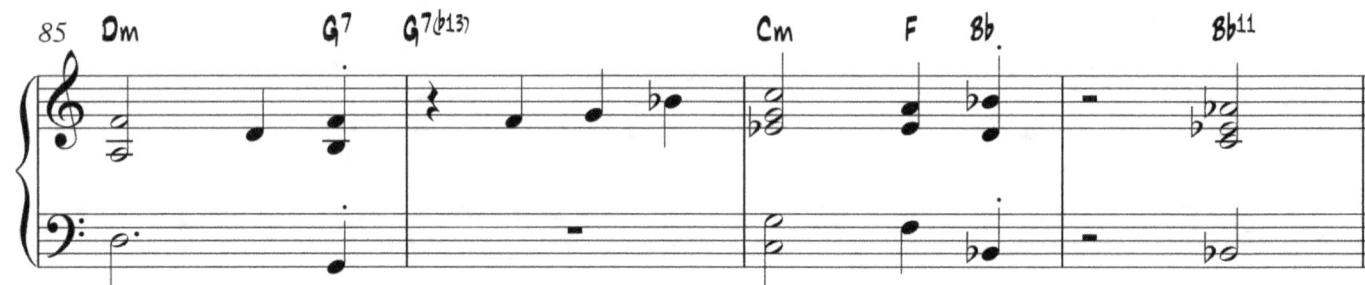

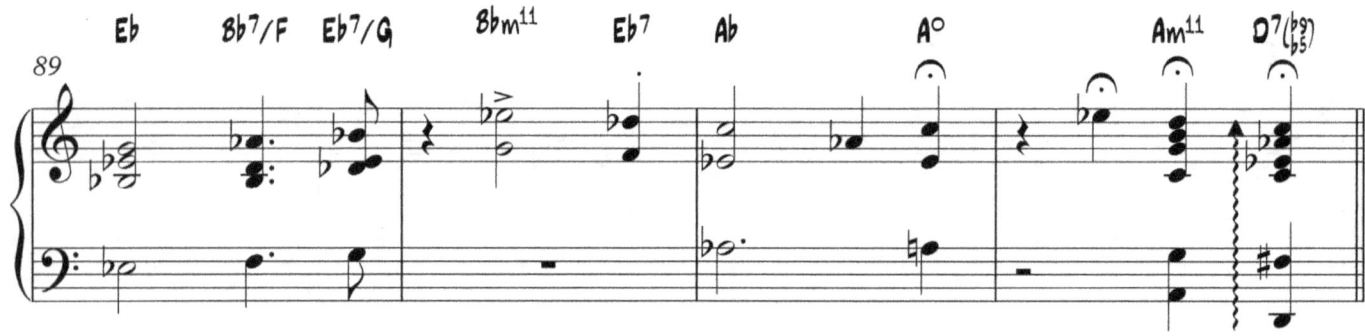

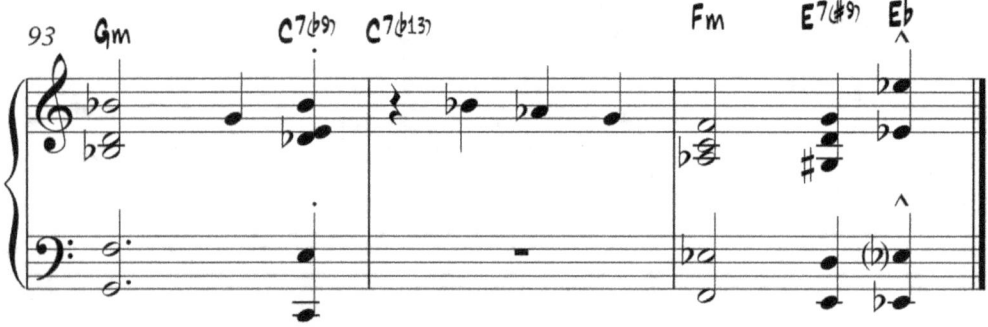

Why do I notate all twelve keys for most of these exercises? Because 12 keys is that important. I'll keep going on about everything in twelve keys until my fingers fall off.

The reason for twelve keys is this: each key signature feels different on a piano. If you only learn your favorite licks and chords in one key, you are selling yourself short because you won't be able to jam on those chords and licks in other keys. This is especially important with vocalists.

On the piano, your fingers (and brain) need to have the feel of all the keys so you can play in all the keys.

Being able to play in all keys is one of the many technical skills that sets apart the professionals from the amateurs, and one of the skills that is easiest to learn if you put the time in.

Calypso Exercise 4

This is a groove exercise in 12 keys.

Once this exercise is part of your groove repository, it can be used in a lot of your music. There's also the cool factor - when you sit down at someone's piano and start jamming on a calypso piano groove people always stop to check it out.

Scot Ranney

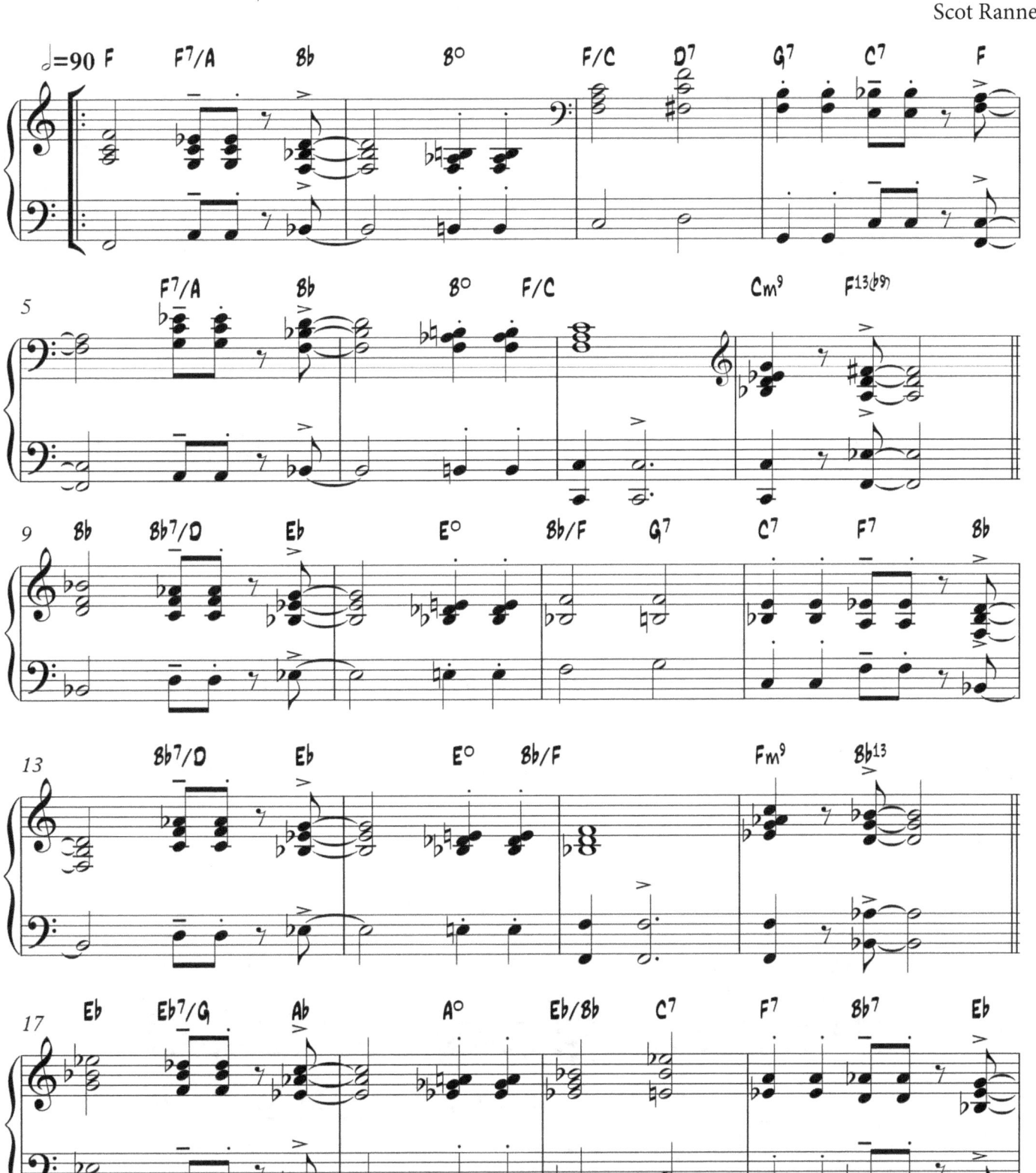

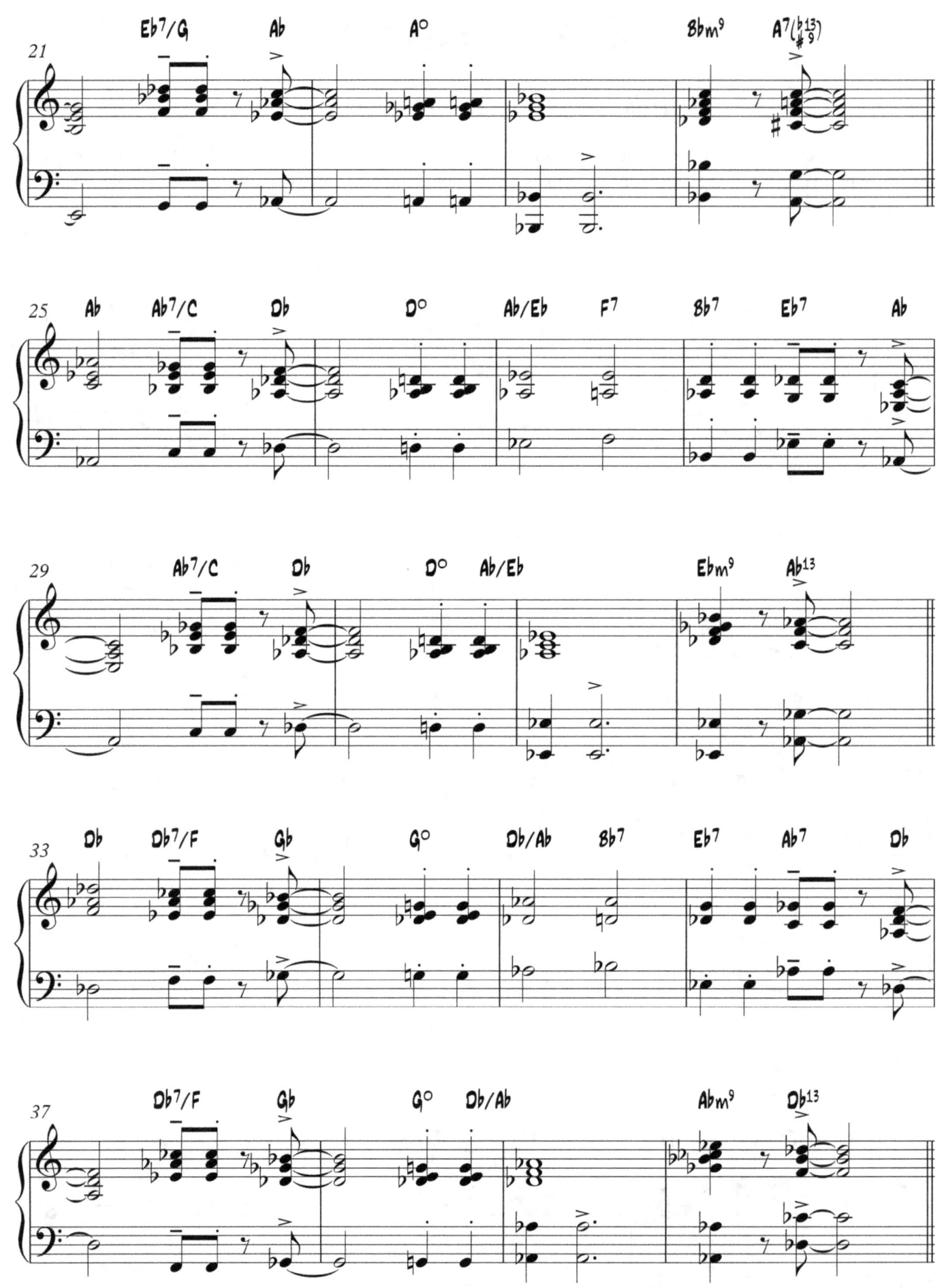

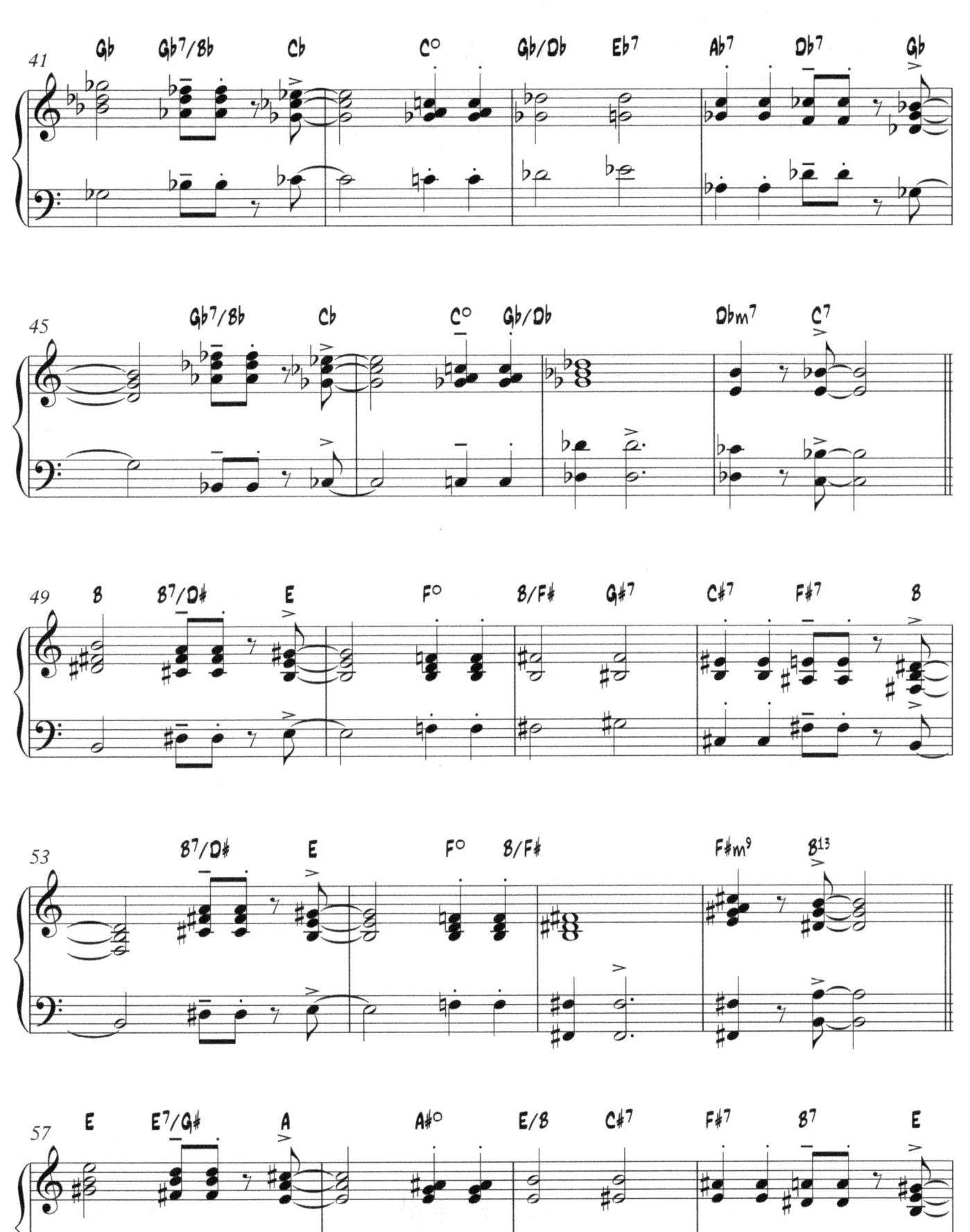

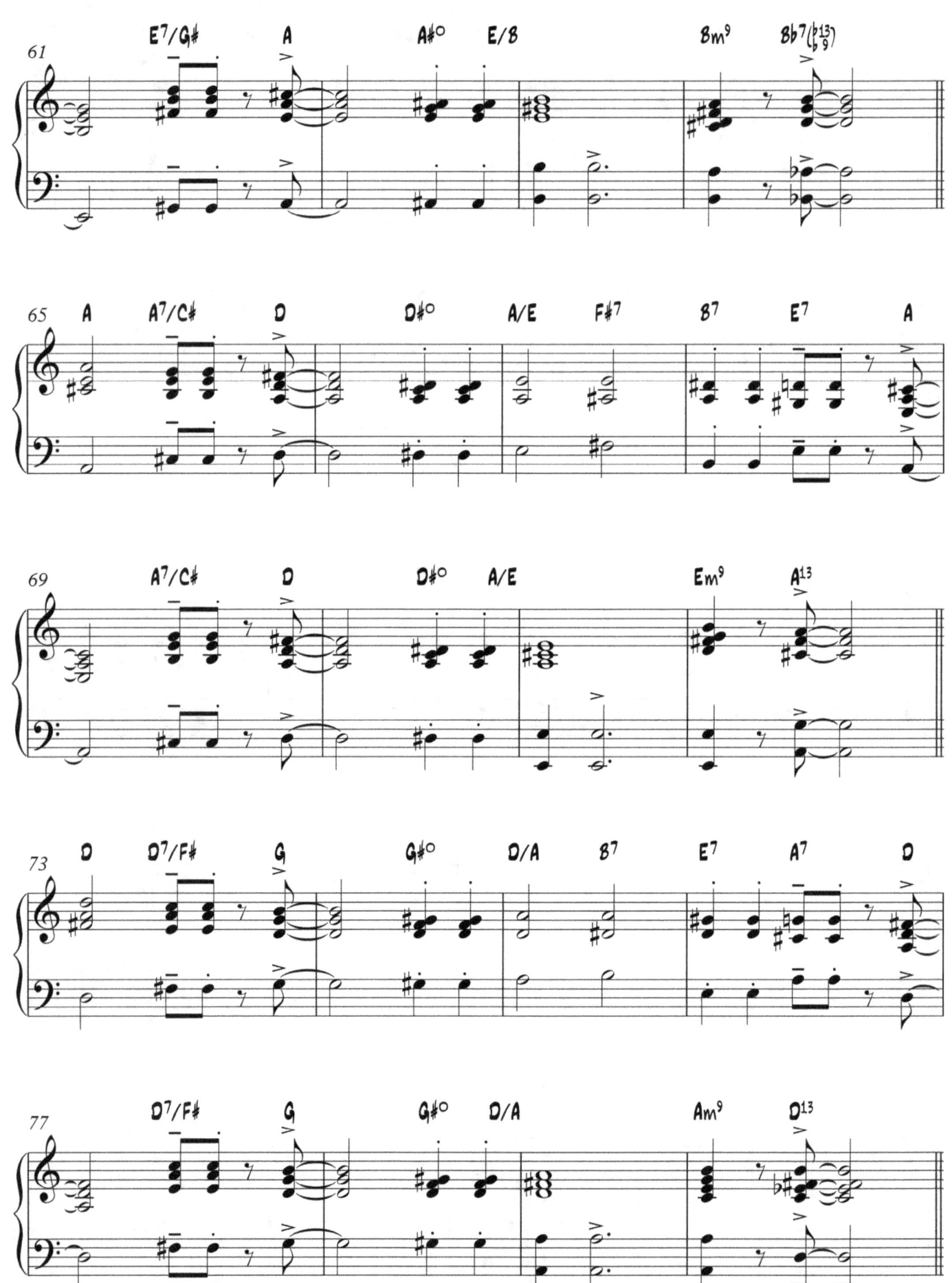

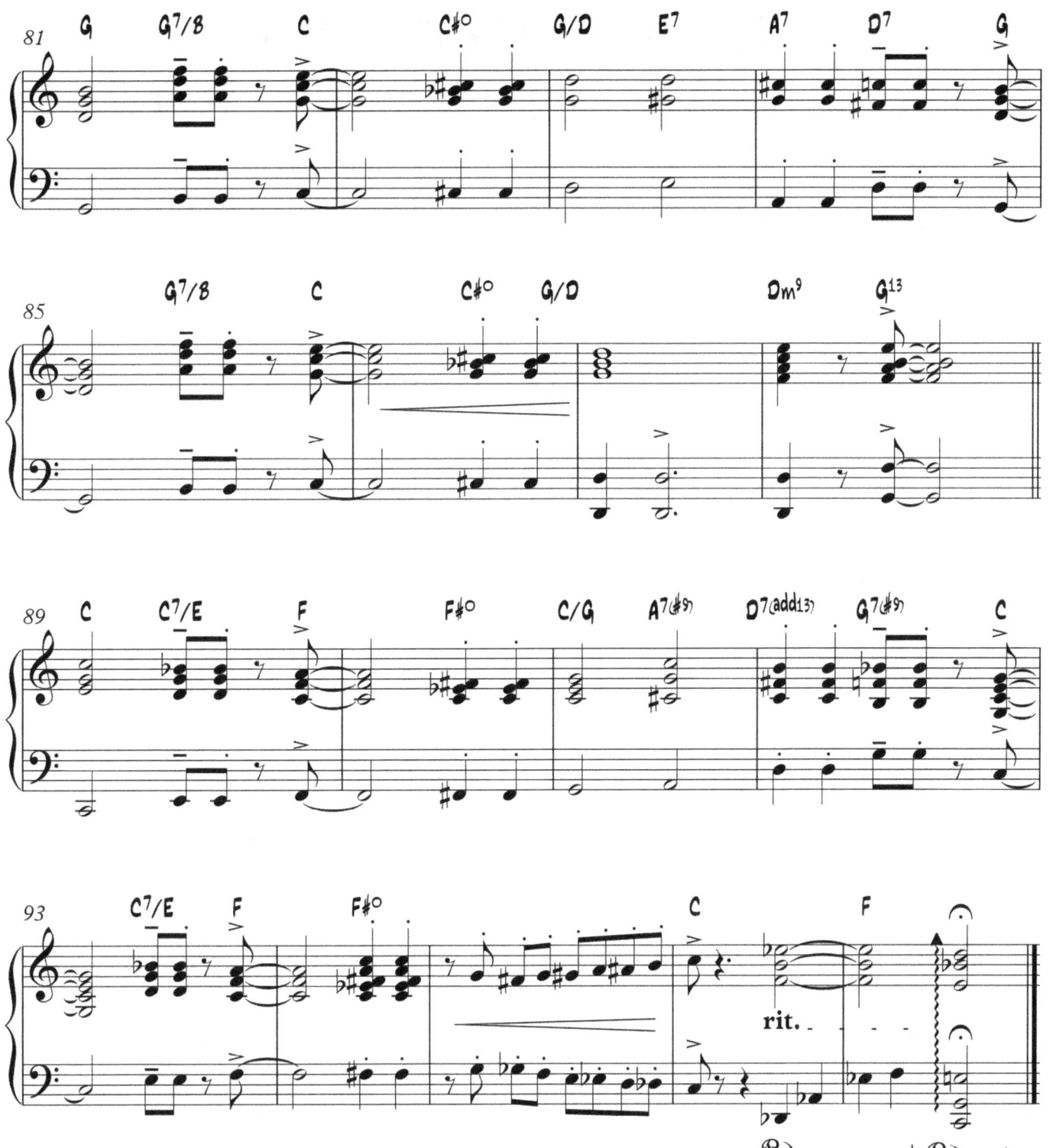

Why write a Cb instead of a B, or an Fb instead of an E? This happens all over the book and the reason is to make sure the notes are reflecting the theory and key of the passage. On stage I wouldn't hand music out like this, but it's important to know what's going on theory-wise when practicing.

Practice from the head, play from the heart.

Technique: Modern Arpeggios

Based on chords from the first 8 bars of the song "On Green Dolphin Street."

Practicing arpeggios leads to monster techique. Chord voicings get burned into your playing, your left hand feels as independent as your right, and the benefits start showing up in your playing faster than expected. About as close to instant gratification as you can get to in jazz piano.

Be precise! Do not practice mistakes. Go slow untl parts are perfect. The fingerings are guidelines only. Use whatever fingerings feel good to you as long as the transitions and hard parts stay smooth.

Pour yourself a cup of Zen tea and get into the groove. You don't have to read the music the whole time, once you have the formula down just play. Use the sustain pedal to bring out the flow of your playing without sounding muddy.

Scot Ranney

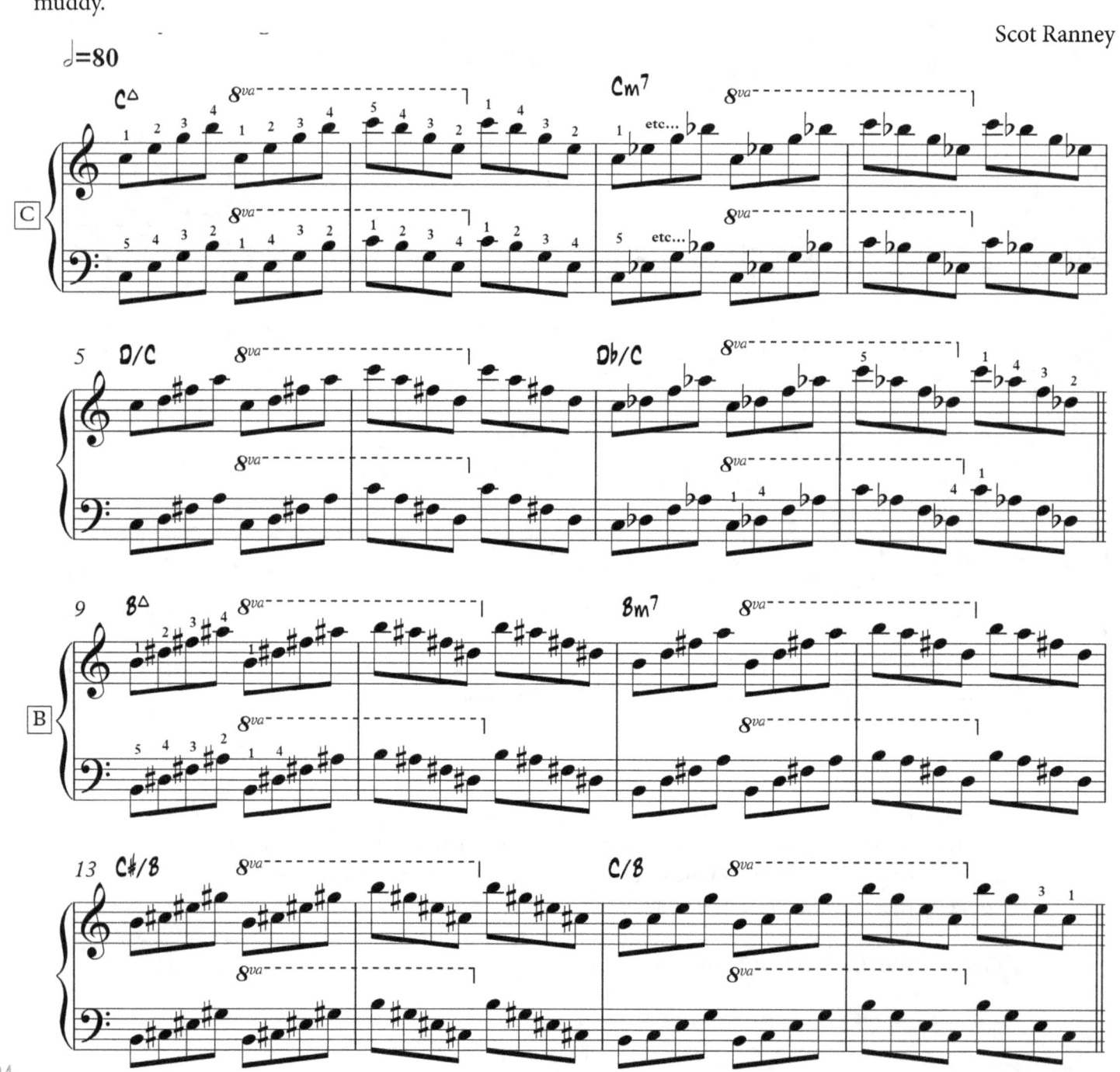

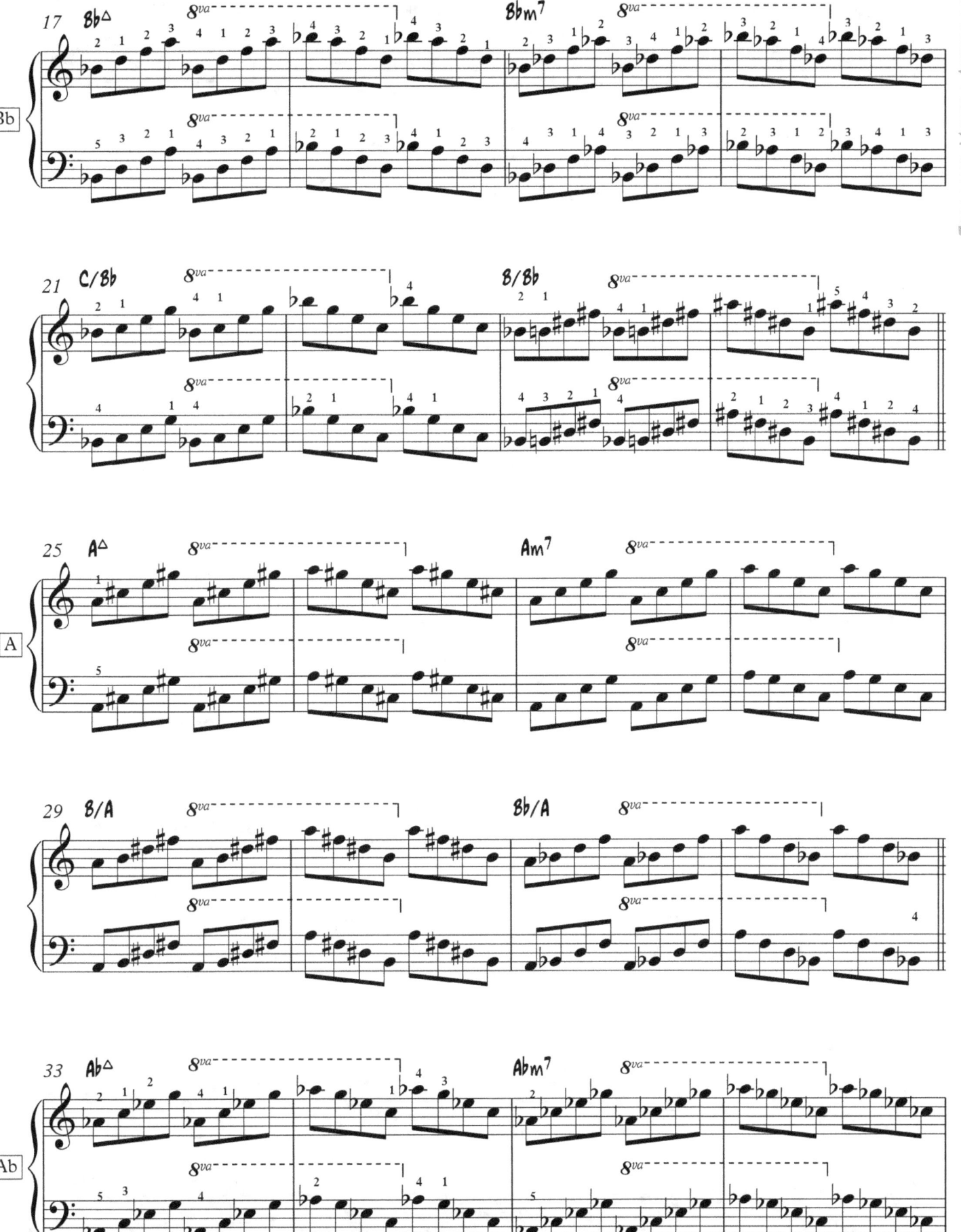

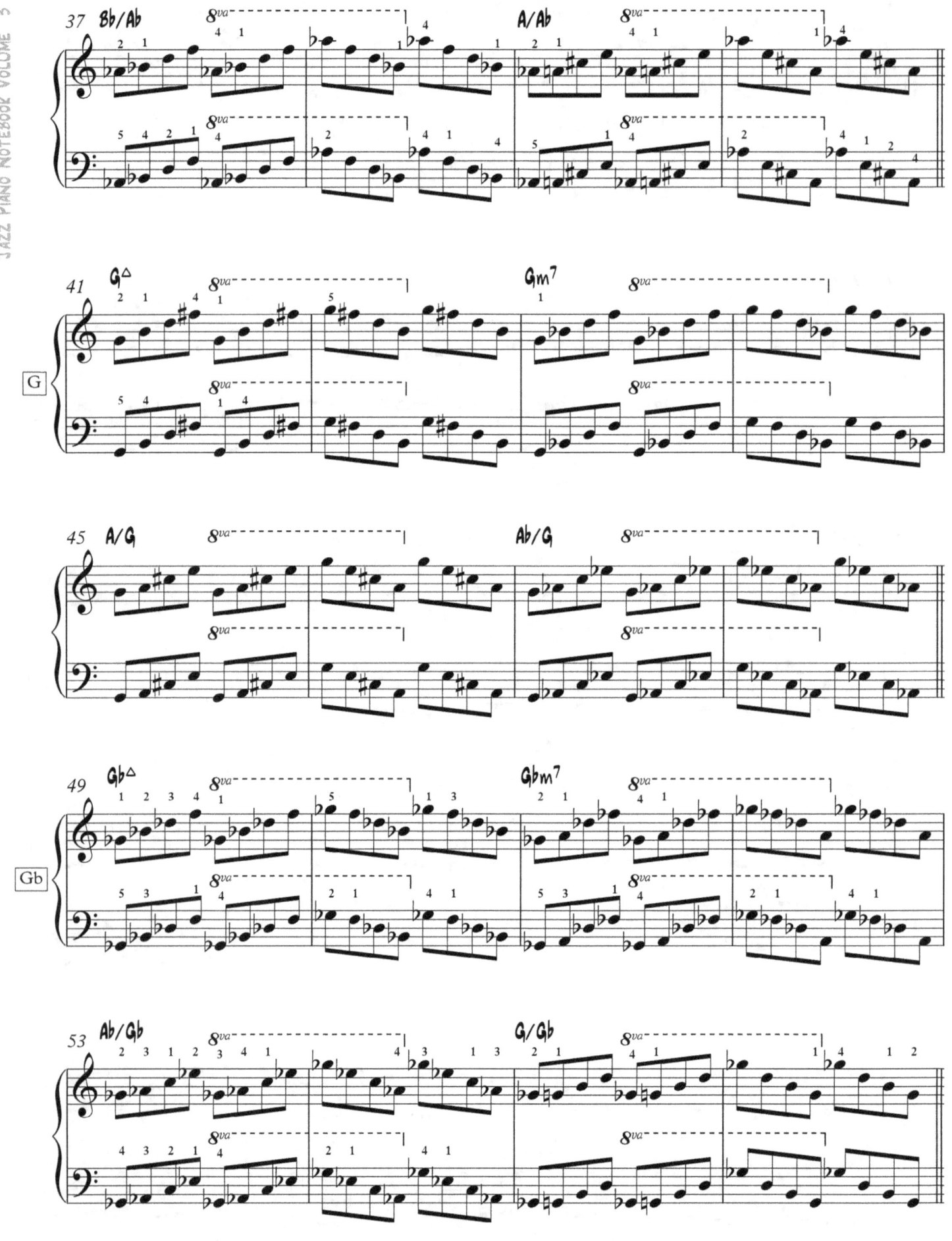

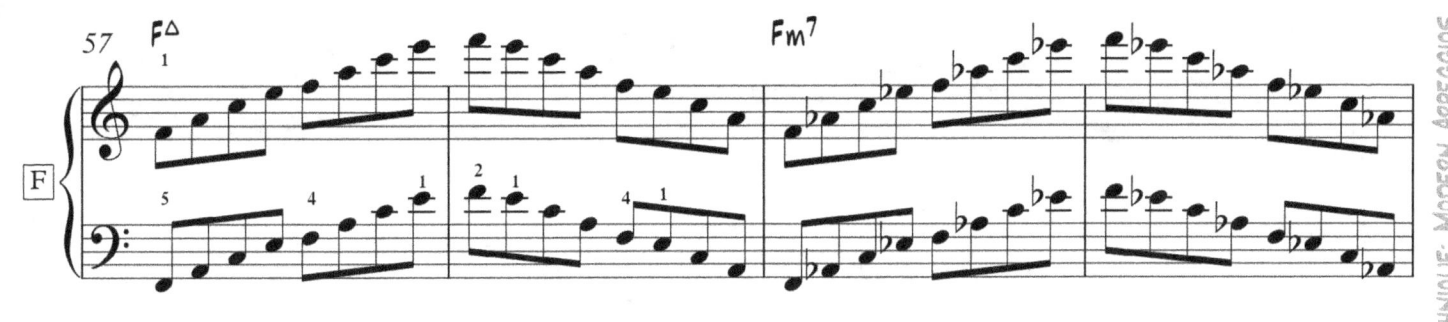

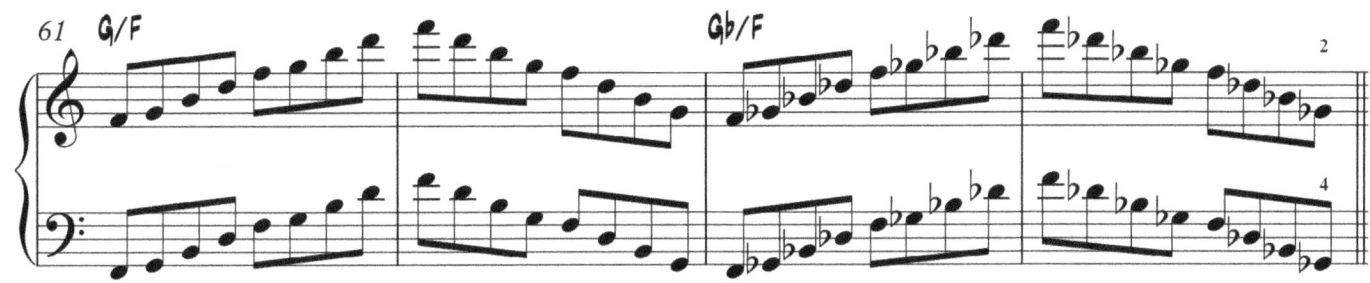

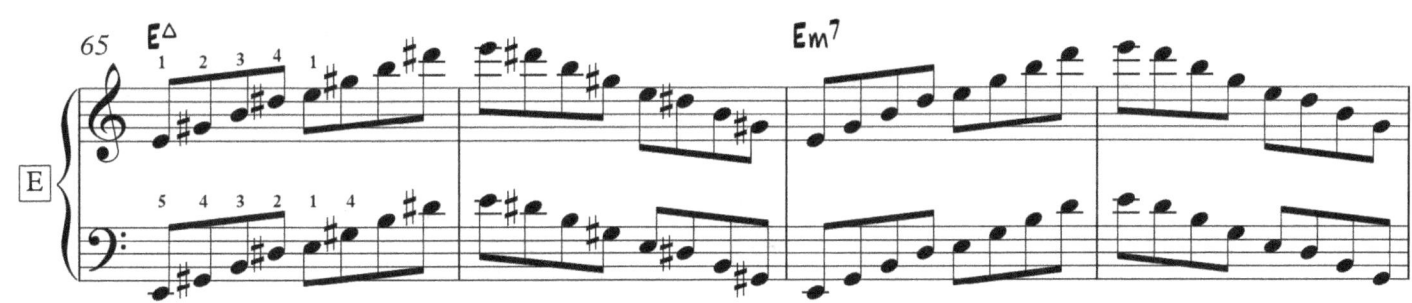

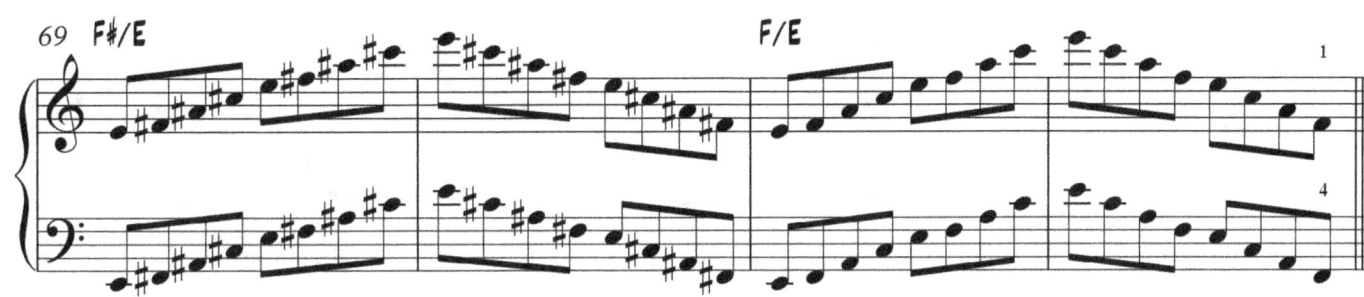

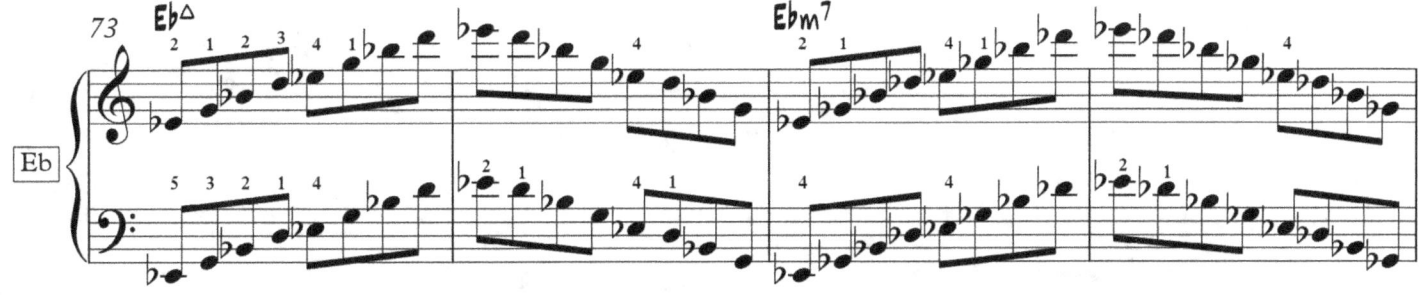

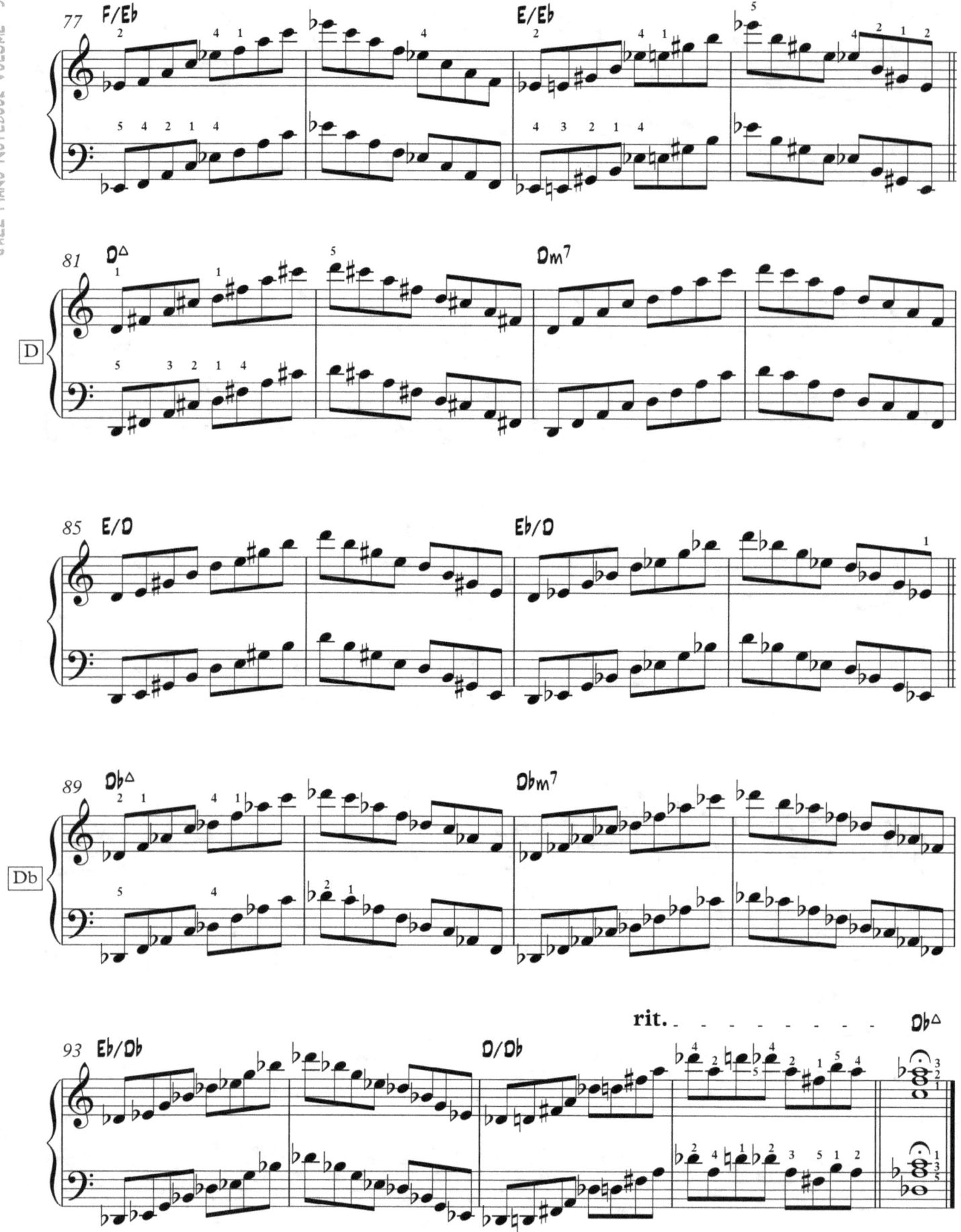

SUSTAIN II–V–I TRANSITION EXERCISE

Sound tasty and create subtle currents of interest with tension and release.

Creative sustain and release transitions is one of the difference makers when it comes to sounding like a professional. You're probably familiar on some level with the 2-5-1 progression. Adding some moving parts to the 2-5-1 sounds sophisticated and pro. The word *tasty* covered in *tasty sauce* comes to mind.

In this exercise, the first chord in each pair is a sus4 that resolves into a 7th chord before finally resolving to the 1 chord. Based on the sound, it's still basically a 2-5-1 chord, and in the end, what it sounds like will always be more important than what it looks like.

Scot Ranney

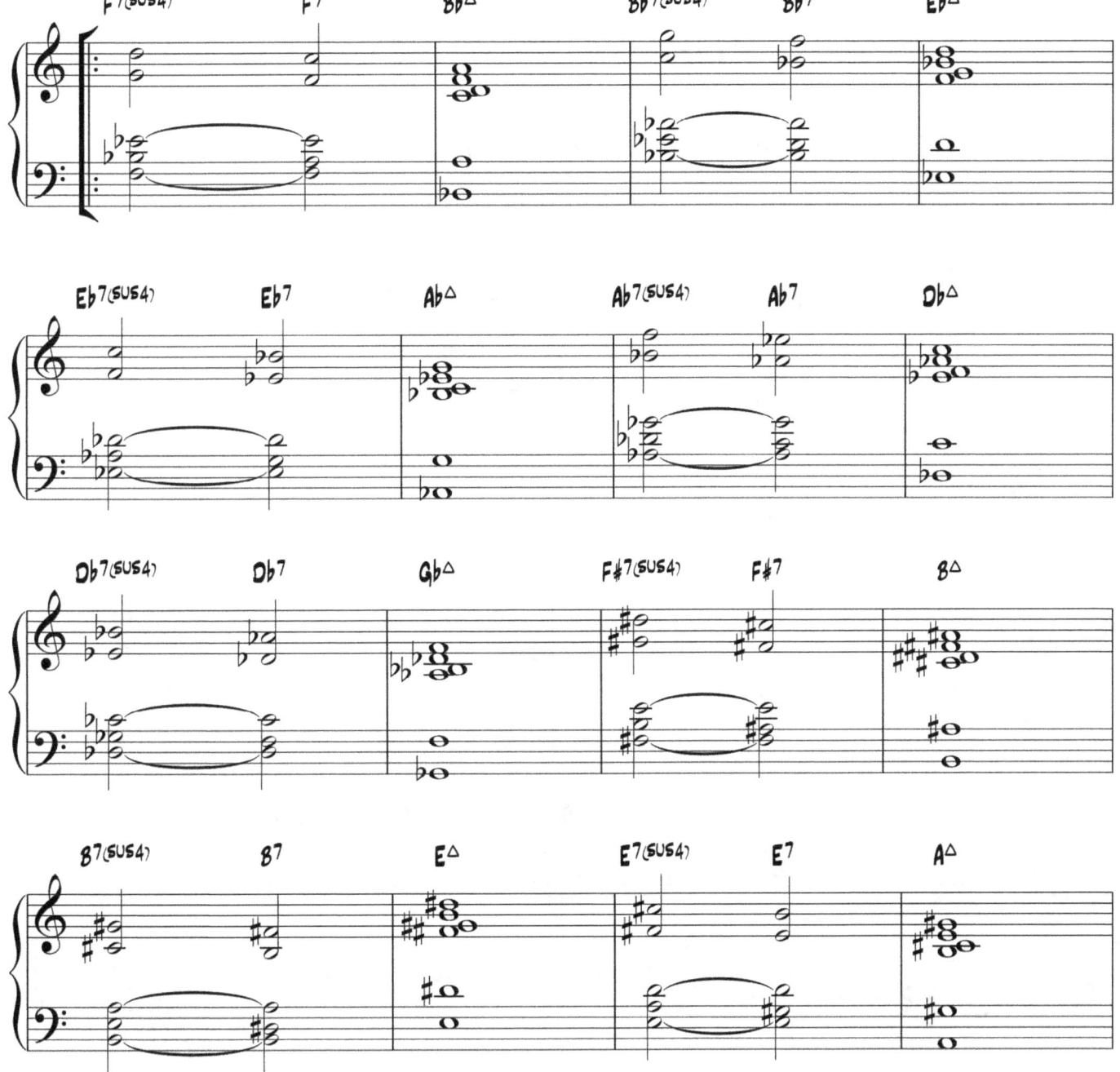

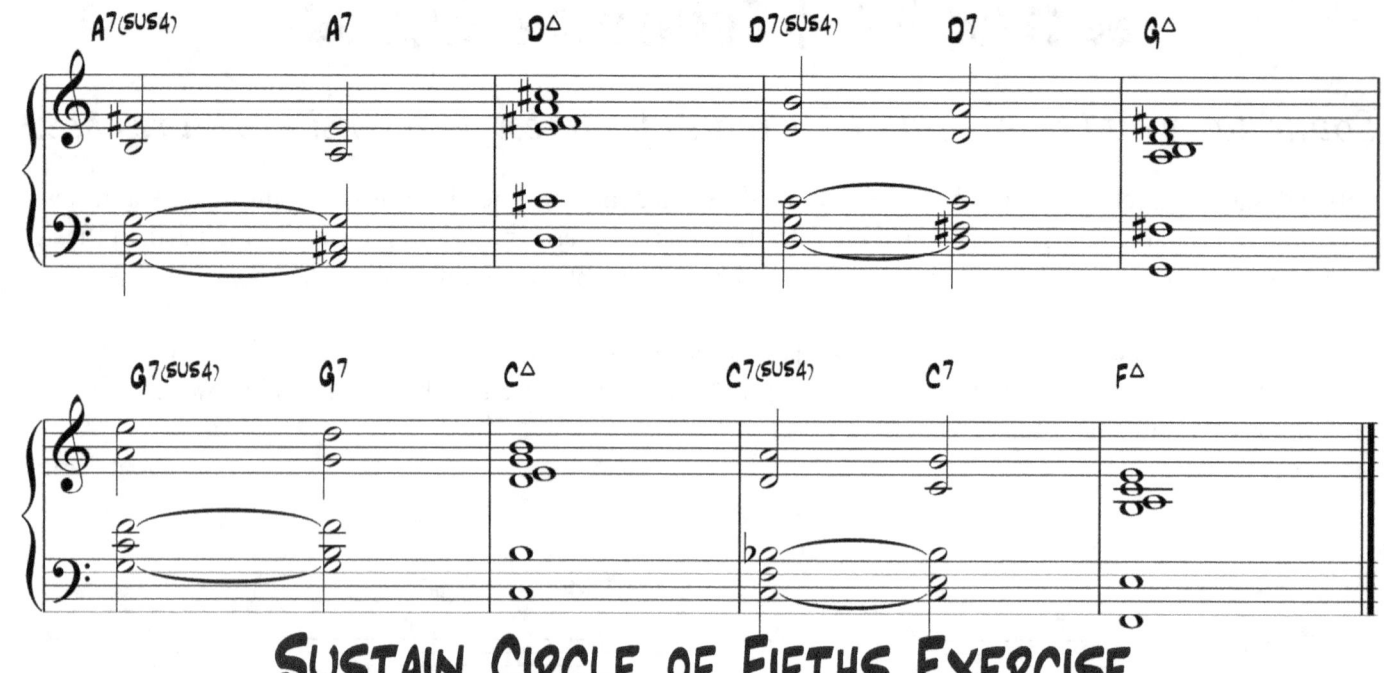

Sustain Circle of Fifths Exercise

The more of this kind of thing the better.

This is a variation of the last study with slightlly different motion and sound.

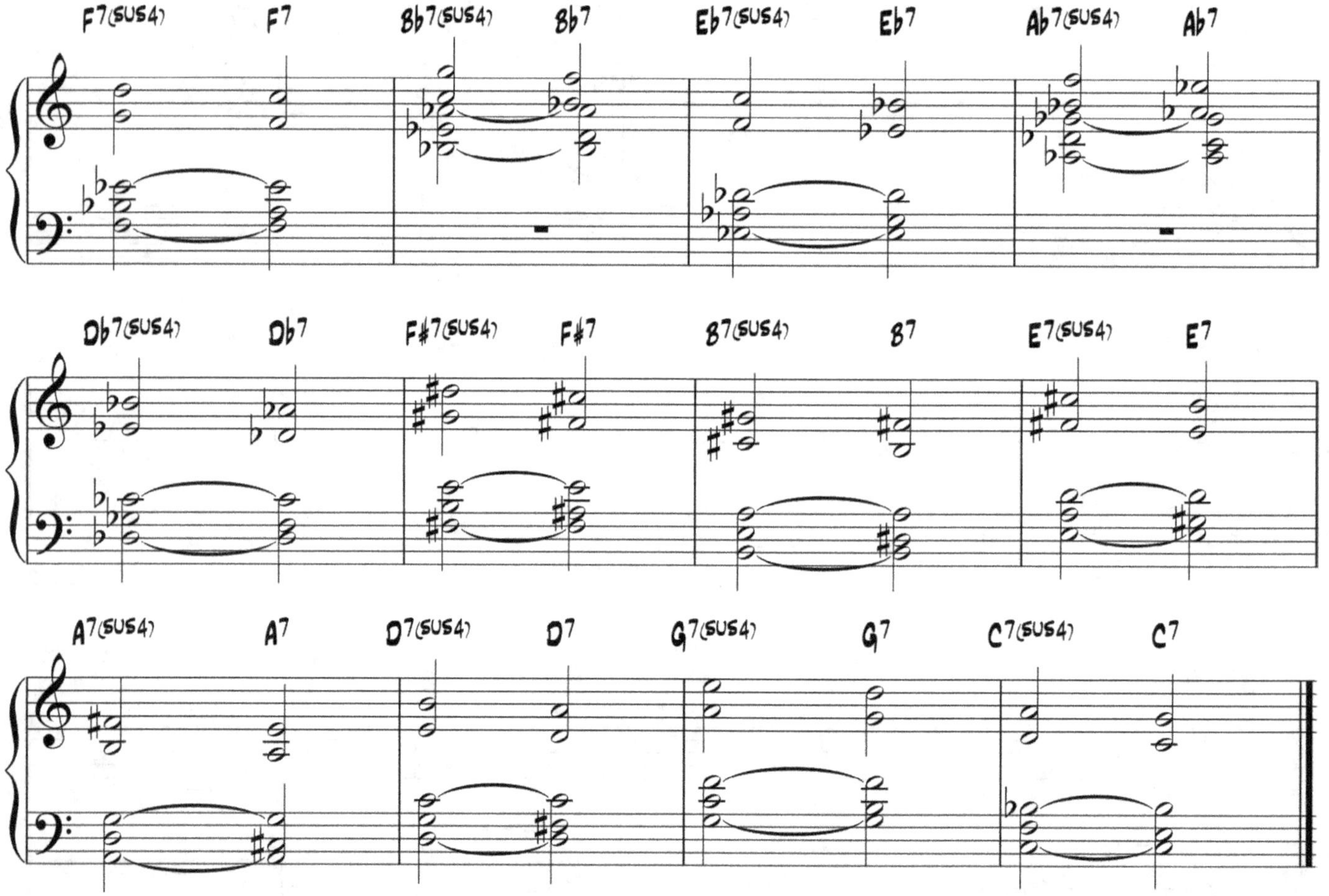

Sustain II-V-I Transition Exercise

This simple idea can put a lot of tools at your fingertips. Tasty tools.

Altering one or two key notes in these progressions will change the mood of the sound quite a bit. Choose your alterations by altered notes in the melody and/or harmony of the song you are playing.

These are all 2-5-1 progressions. It's important to see these kinds of progressions in a song because they are mini-harmonic centers. If you know the harmonic centers of a song it's easier to improvise because harmonically there are no mysteries. All you have to do is jam and have fun making music without trying to overthink the chord changes.

Scot Ranney

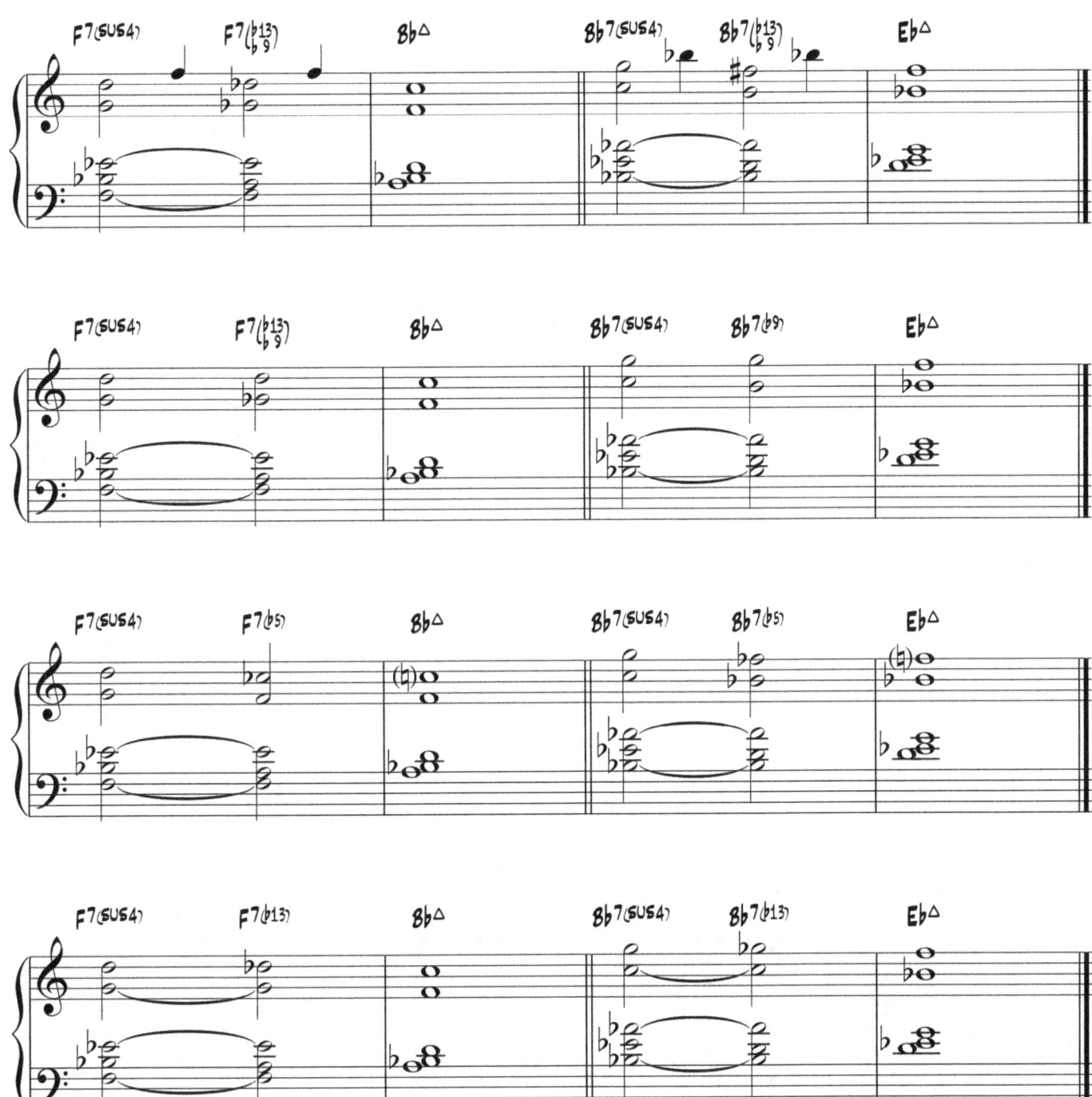

Sustain Example 1 - Body and Soul: Use of the flat 13 variation in the middle of the second bar. This variation fist into the V-I (Ab to Db) and sets up the next melody note (F) perfectly. This adds some tasty playing to your ballads and medium tempo songs.

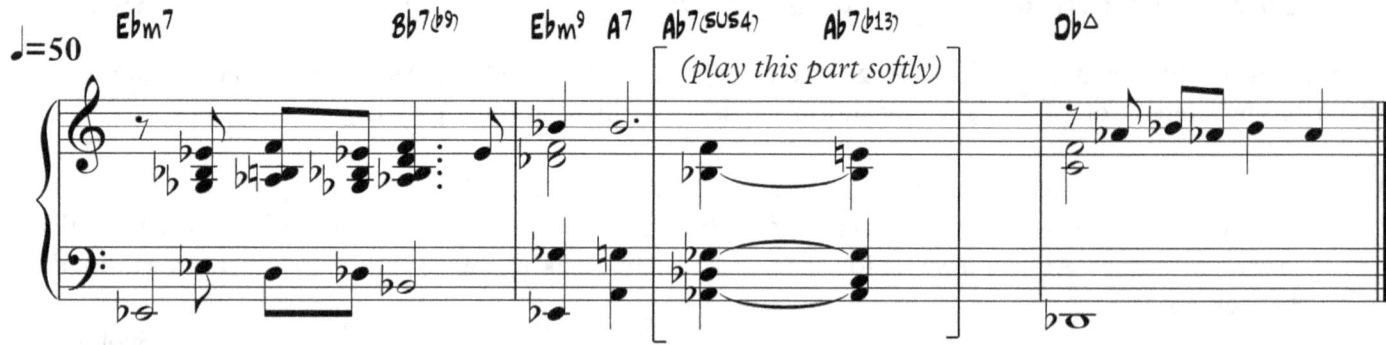

Sustain Example 2 - Cry Me A River: When using these kinds of sustain/release techniques, keep the melody of the song in the foreground and the harmonies in the background. One reason this work so well when Keith Jarret does it his full command of how loud each of his fingers play. If you can control the volume of each note in a chord you can control an entirely new layer of your music.

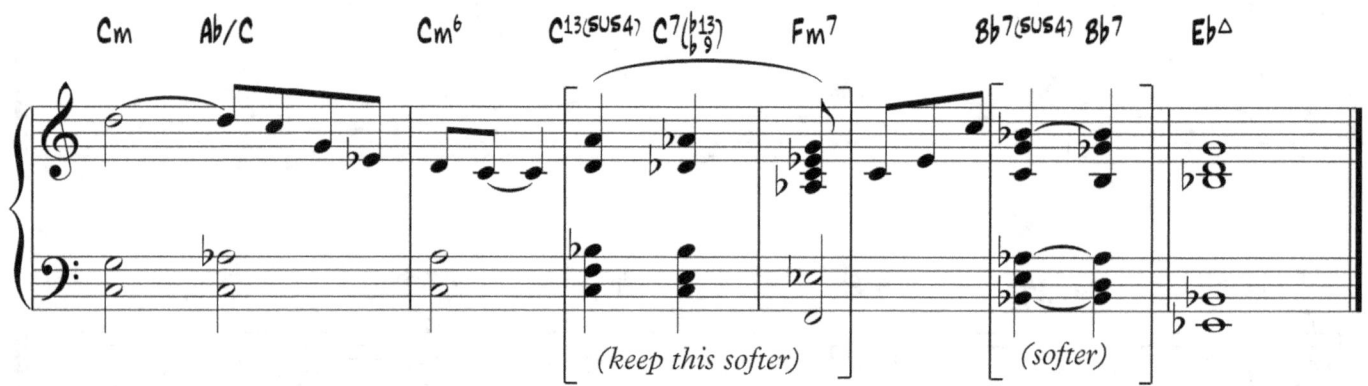

Sustain Example 3 - A Nightengale Sang in Barkley Square

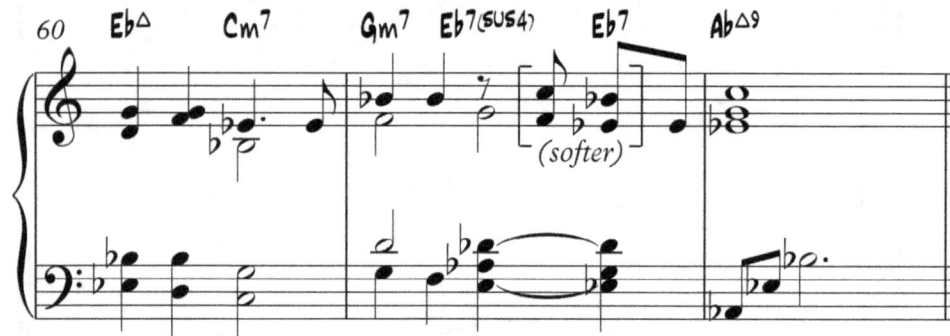

Bring the melody out and hold long notes fully. The more subtle the transition notes are, the more effective and natural they will sound.

Careful and detailed practice without glossing over will get this stuff in your fingers much faster than practicing it wrong.

Sustain Example 4 - I Thought About You

The snippet below starts on bar 5 of the song, this technique starts in bar 8. Any time you have long notes in the melody you can explore ways to use this kind of inside counterpoint-like melodic motion.

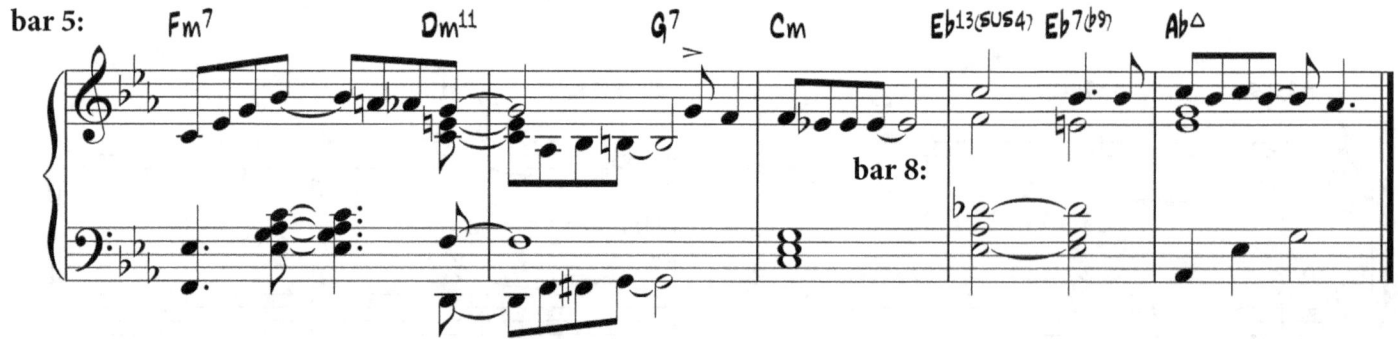

Four Variations on a Calypso Groove

Four ways to make your fingers dance.

Listen to a Michel Camilo song called, "Why Not" to get an idea of where you can go with this kind of groove.

Michel Camilo was my first high energy Latin jazz piano influence. His playing attracted me because of how well he utilizes rhythm and how funky that makes his playing. He also has great technique and his energy is contagious. All of my favorite piano players have that in common- great time, energy, strength to play the piano as a percussion instrument, and they always have fun.

Scot Ranney

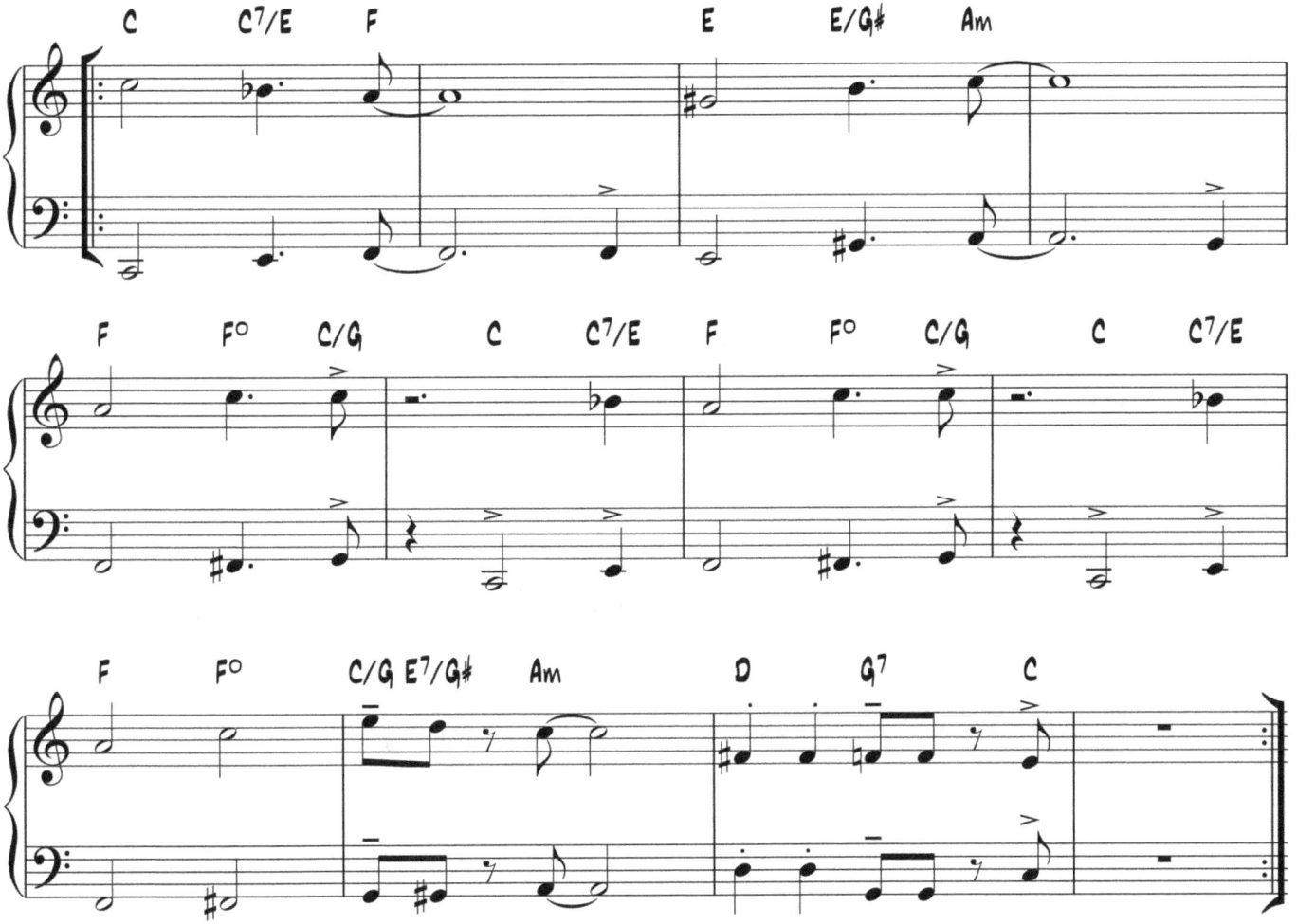

"If you play a tune and a person don't tap their feet, don't play the tune."

~ Count Basie

VARIATION 2

Gospelly goodness.

The voicings used in this variation add a gospelly touch to the groove. Play it with some punch as if the chords were horn sections made of deaf trumpet players who need to play loud. There is also a rhythmic addition starting in the second line.

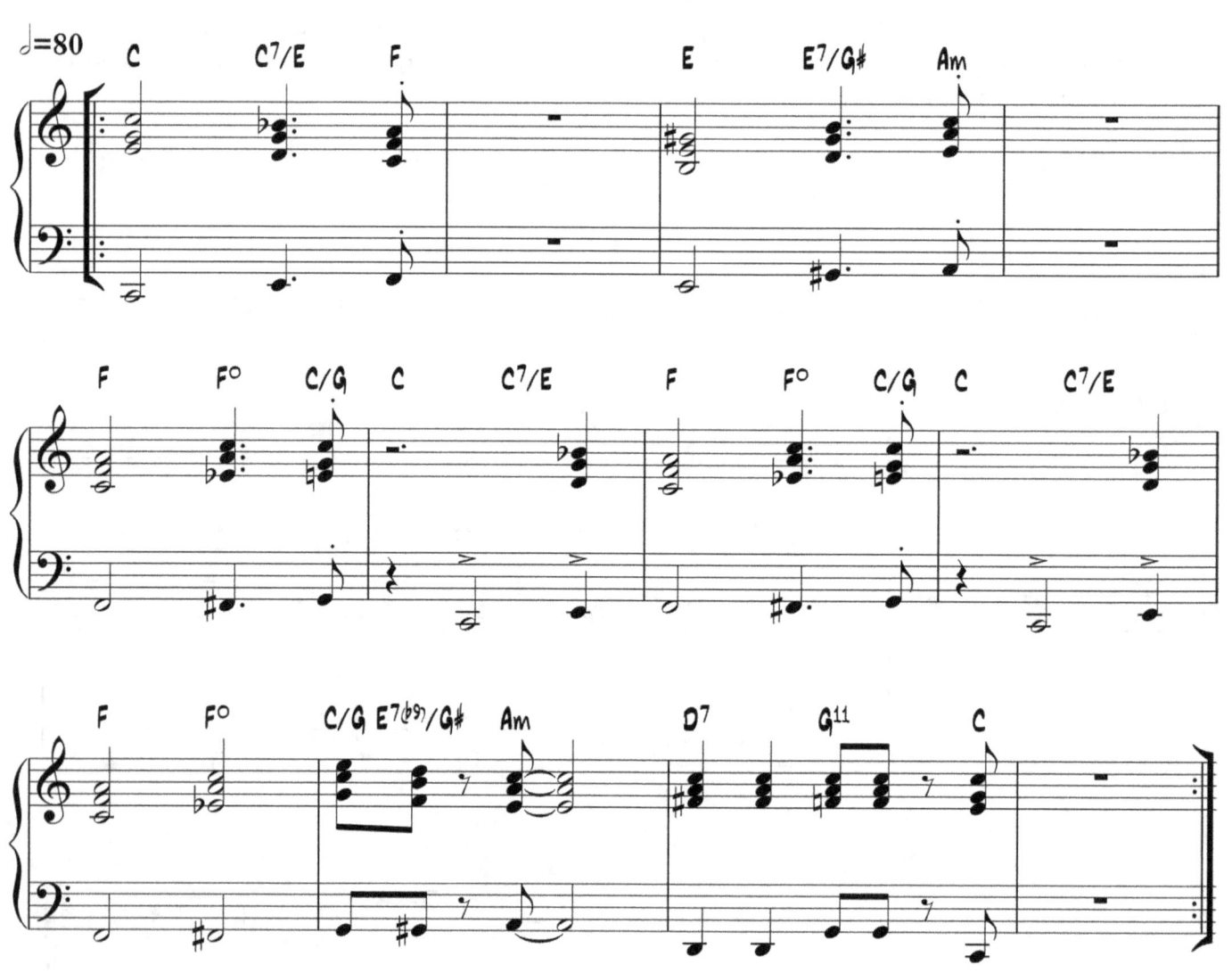

"There is no such thing as a wrong note."

~ Art Tatum

Variation 3

Pseudo-Montuno

Here we will add a touch of arpeggiation to give the groove more flavor. In this kind of Latin jazz groove, chords can be arpeggiated to add more rhythm and interest, and in some cases are required for particular latin jazz styles. Check out Rebeca Mauleon's "101 Montunos" for this kind of playing!

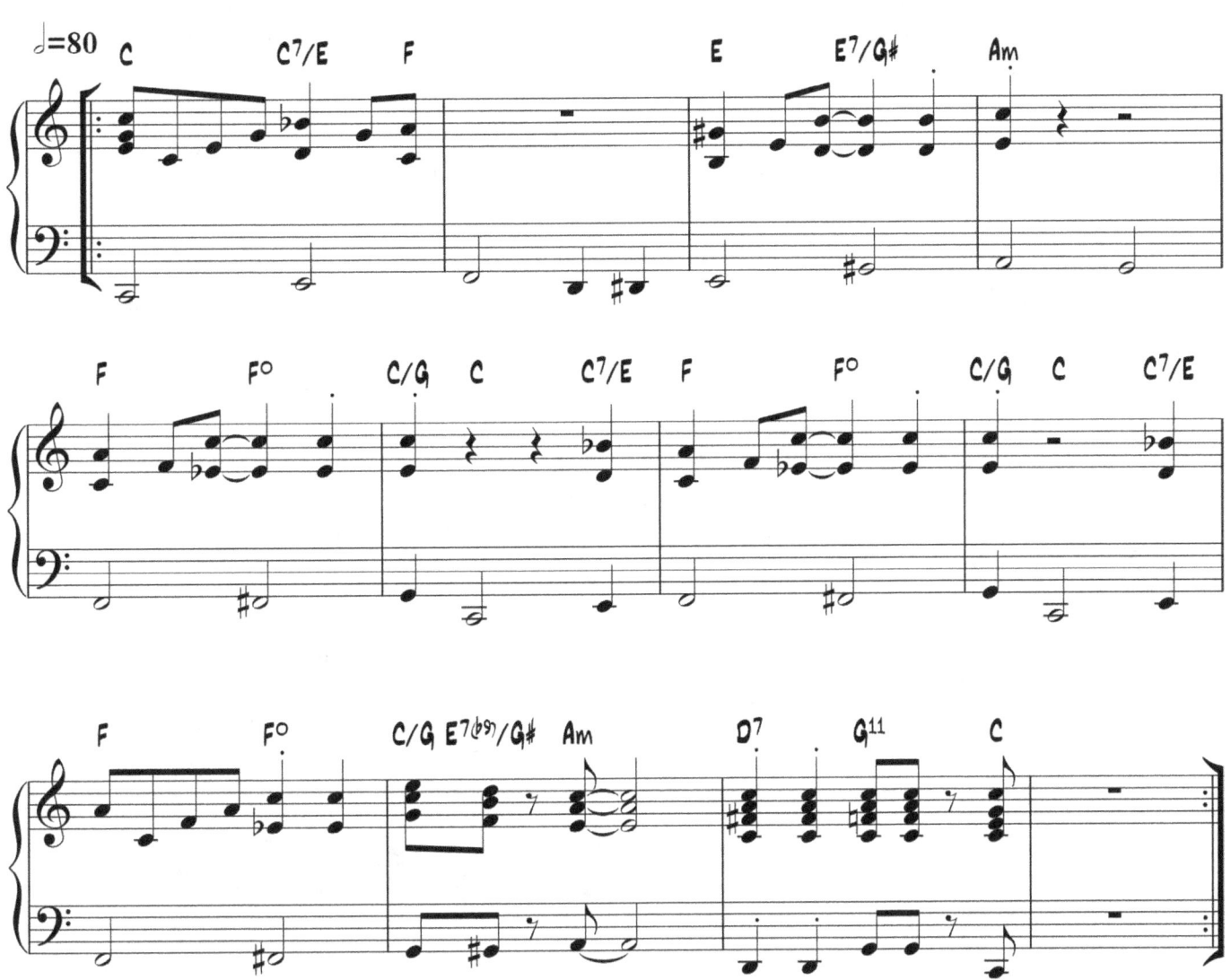

"It's not the note you play that's the wrong note - it's the note you play afterwards that makes it right or wrong."

~ Miles Davis

VARIATION 4

Take it to the next level.

This variation is harmonically based off the others, however larger chords and increased left hand bass complexity add depth and funkyness. There's bit of a ragtime feel at times as well.

The left hand bass lines should be accented when they are by themselves, such as when it leads into E in the third measure and when it leads into F at the beginning of the second line. This helps bring out the counterpoint rhythm in the right hand.

All of these variations should be explored in more than just one key. Your fingers need to know the feeling of the key you are in regardless what key you're in, and the best way to do that is learn songs, grooves, and licks in all keys, all the time.

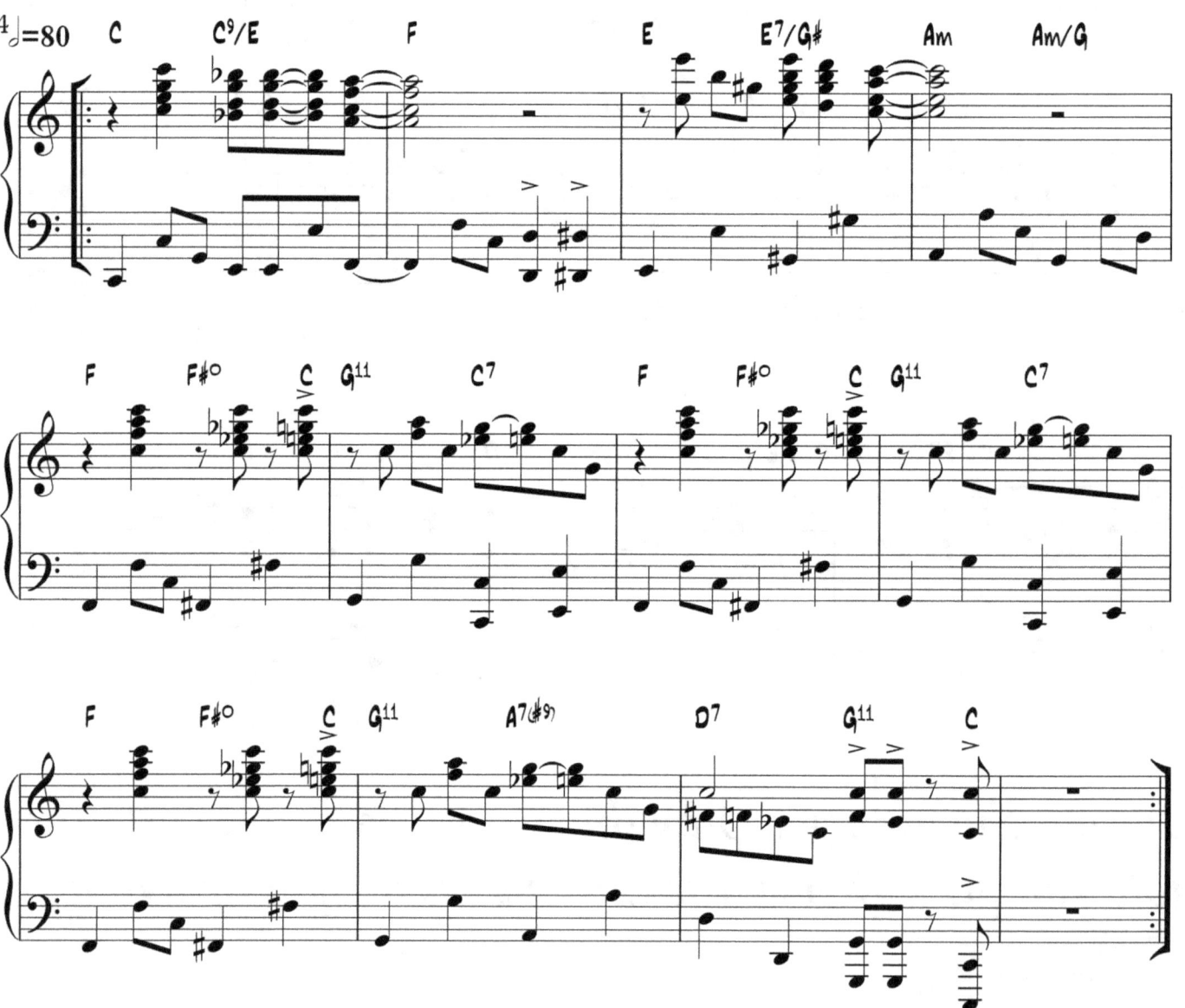

SCALES: CALYPSO STYLE!

If you don't like scales, you're in the wrong business.

My inspiration for calypso jazz, or as I overheard Ray Brown call it at a Jazz Alley concert in Seattle, "coconut jazz," is from the music of Monty Alexander and Michel Camilo. Early Camilo was my first Latin piano influence because of how strong and rhythmically he played. Monty Alexander is the same in that regard, except I first knew him for his epic swing playing from the recording, "Montreux Alexander - Live at the Montreux Jazz Festival". It wasn't until I bought a few more Monty CDs that I heard him play his signature tune, "Funji Mama", an epic "coconut jazz" tune. Check out the great CD "Triple Treat" with Herb Ellis and Ray Brown, as well as these other incredible Monty recordings - "Facets", "Triple Treat", "Ivory and Steel", "Kingston Express" - and others that feature a lot of "coconut jazz".

Scot Ranney

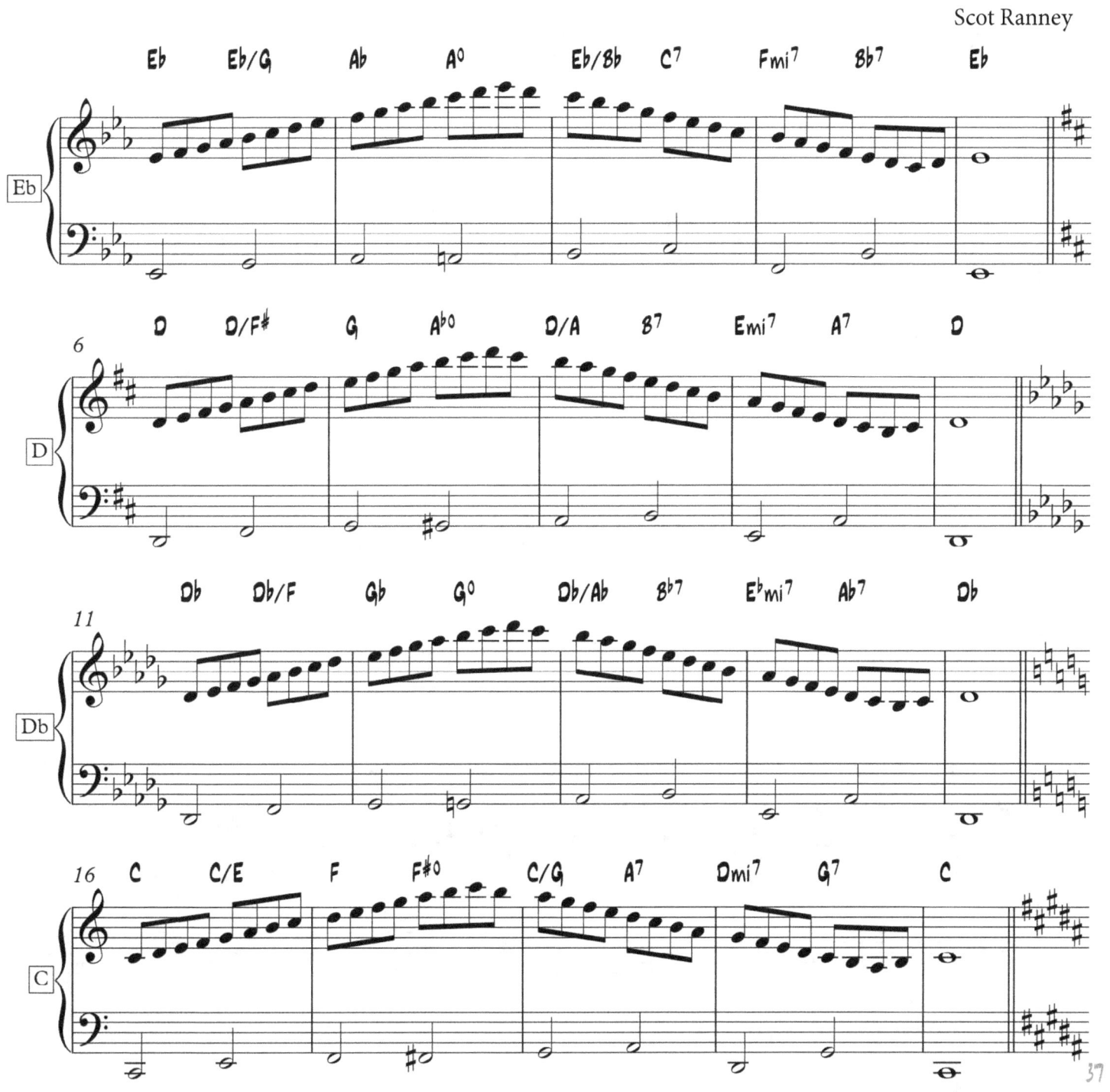

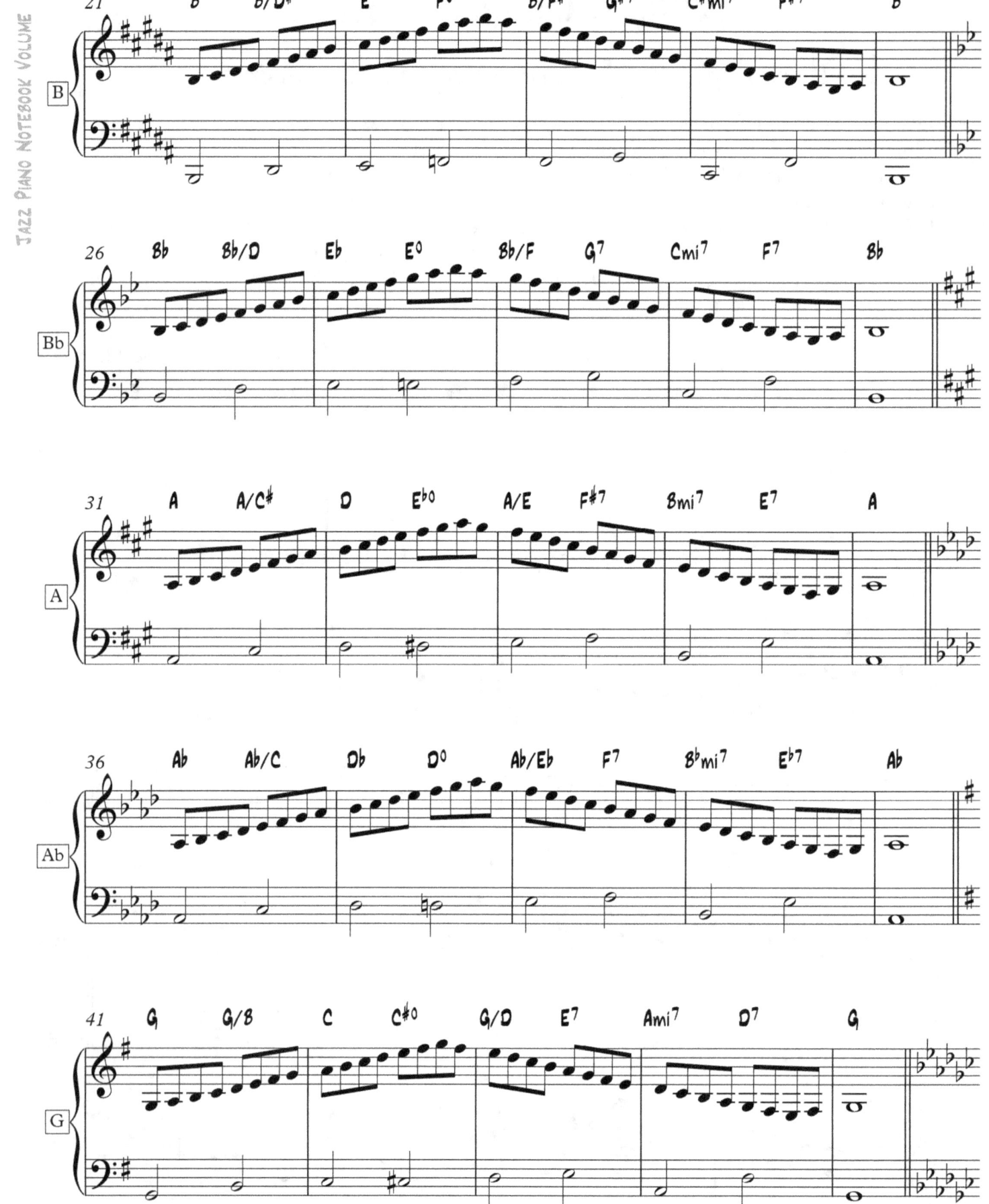

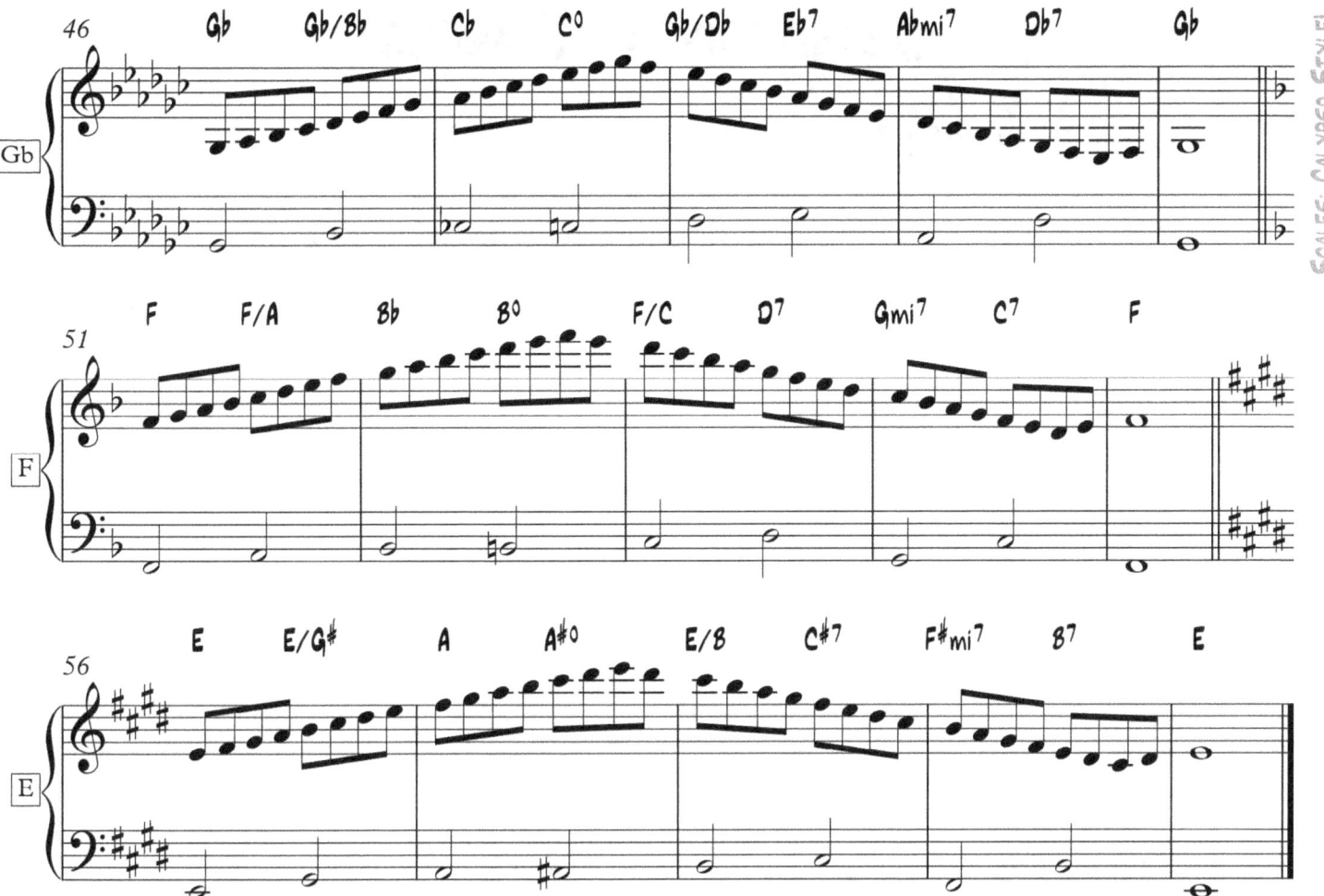

We are in the Golden Age, the Renaissance, of learning musical languages.

Young musicians are better than ever and this is affectng everything in the jazz scene.

Why is this? Consider that at any moment I can watch a Chic Corea or Oscar Peterson concert, I can watch a Montreaux jam session or a George Cables master class, I can listen in on interviews with Count Basie and Duke Ellington.

For all it's hideous brain cell melting poison - there are more searches for "cats videos" than "jazz" - YouTube has also brought us more musical resources than have *ever been available* in the history of humankind.

Music is language, jazz improvisation is conversation

You don't learn a language by sitting around reading a book, you learn it by having conversations and listening to people talk. That's why going to YouTube works. Sit down at your piano and start playing along. Keep it simple at first then figure out the form, the chords, some melody, and then jam with the recording.

Too hard? Don't worry about it, it gets easier. Plow through it. Just do it. Your ears will get stronger faster than you can imagine, and the language of the music you're learning, the style, will become a part of you like you've known it forever. It's really that simple.

Don't get discouraged, start simple and work your way into more complicated songs.

Island Rhythm Changes

Make this one peppy, bouncy, speed it up a notch so it moves.

This is a basic calypso riff that's been expanded a bit with extra chords and rhythms. Think about fun in the sun while playing it, try jamming on it. The basic chord structure is C rhythm changes with an ascending bass line.

Scot Ranney

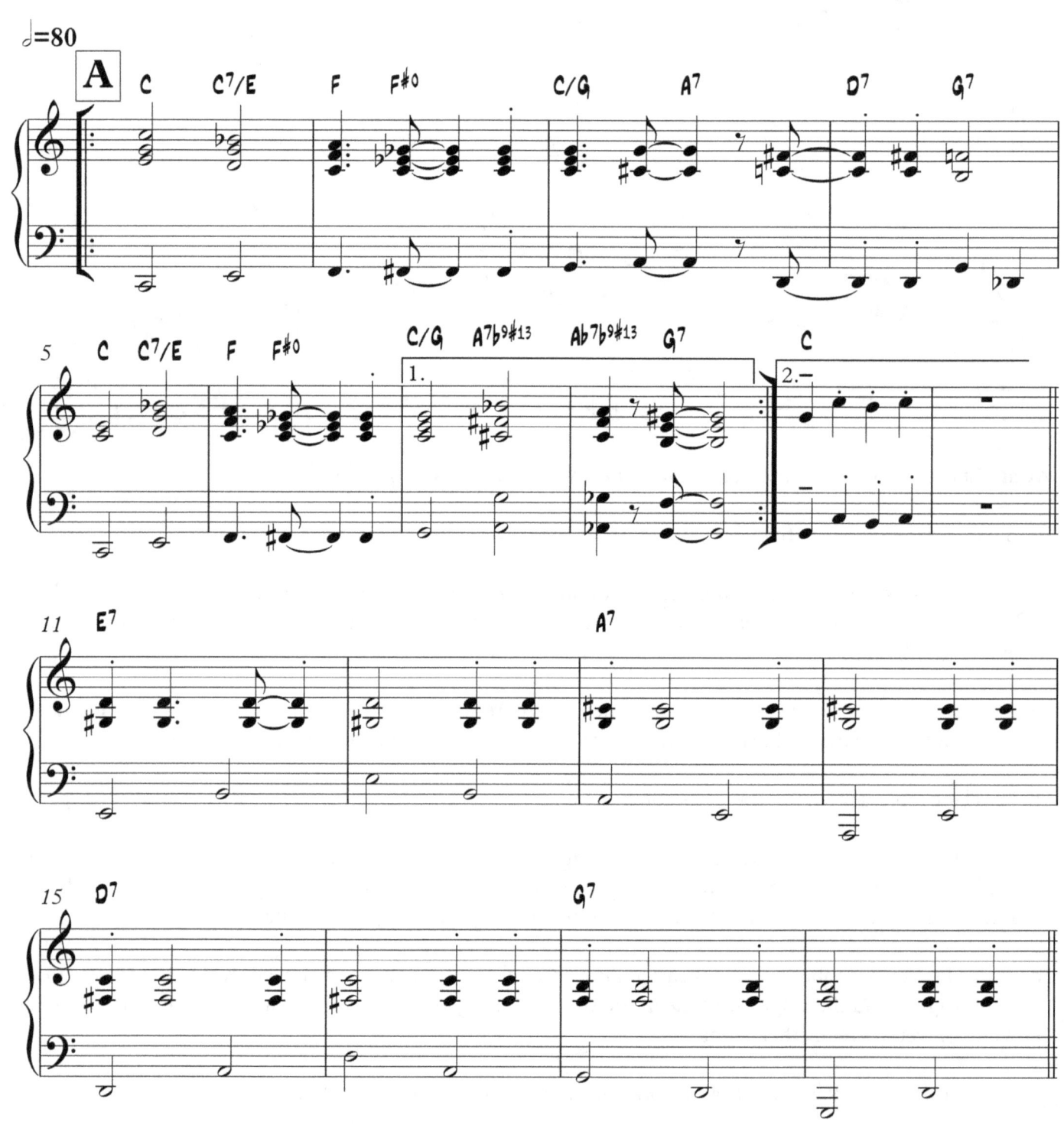

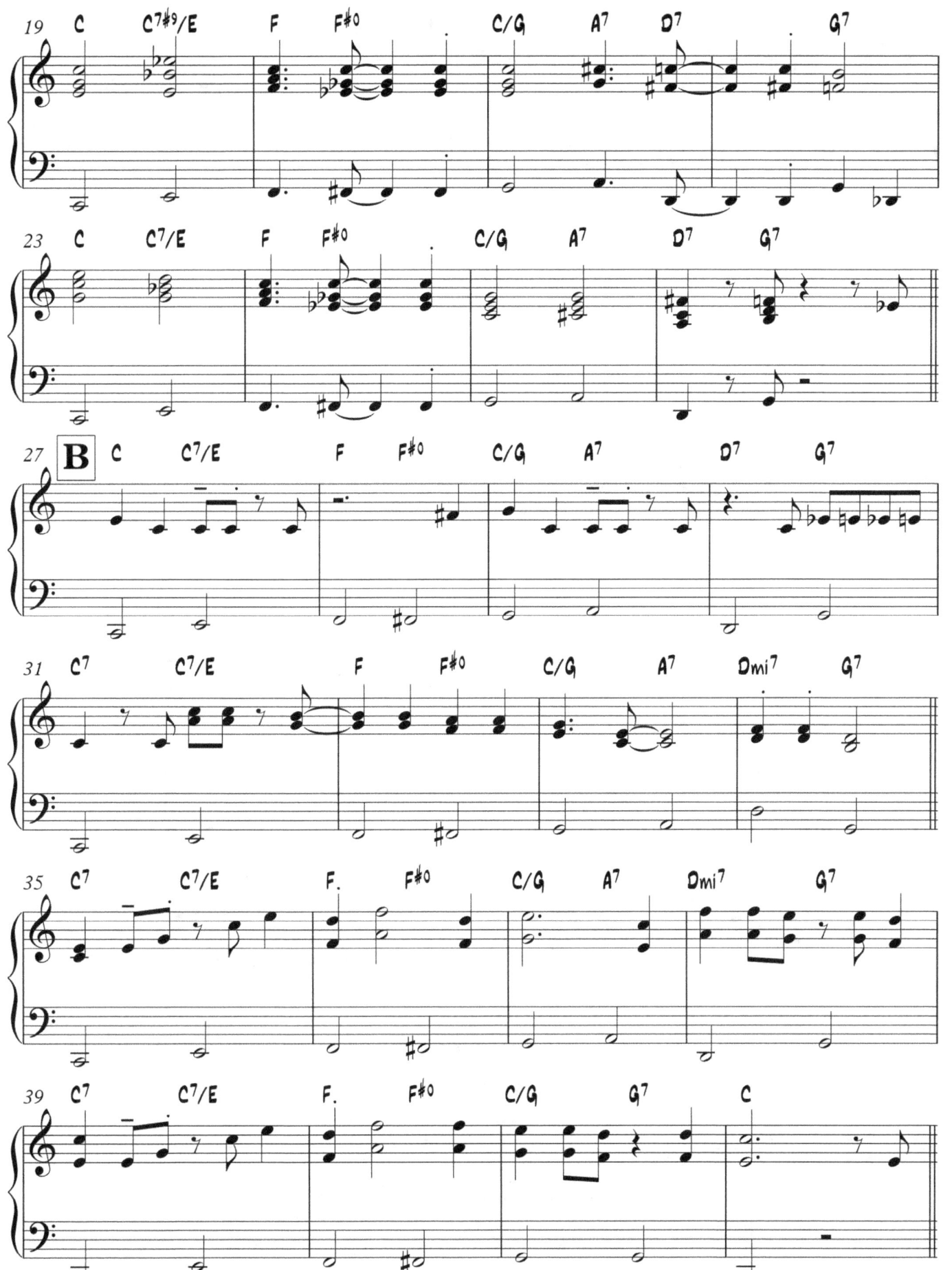

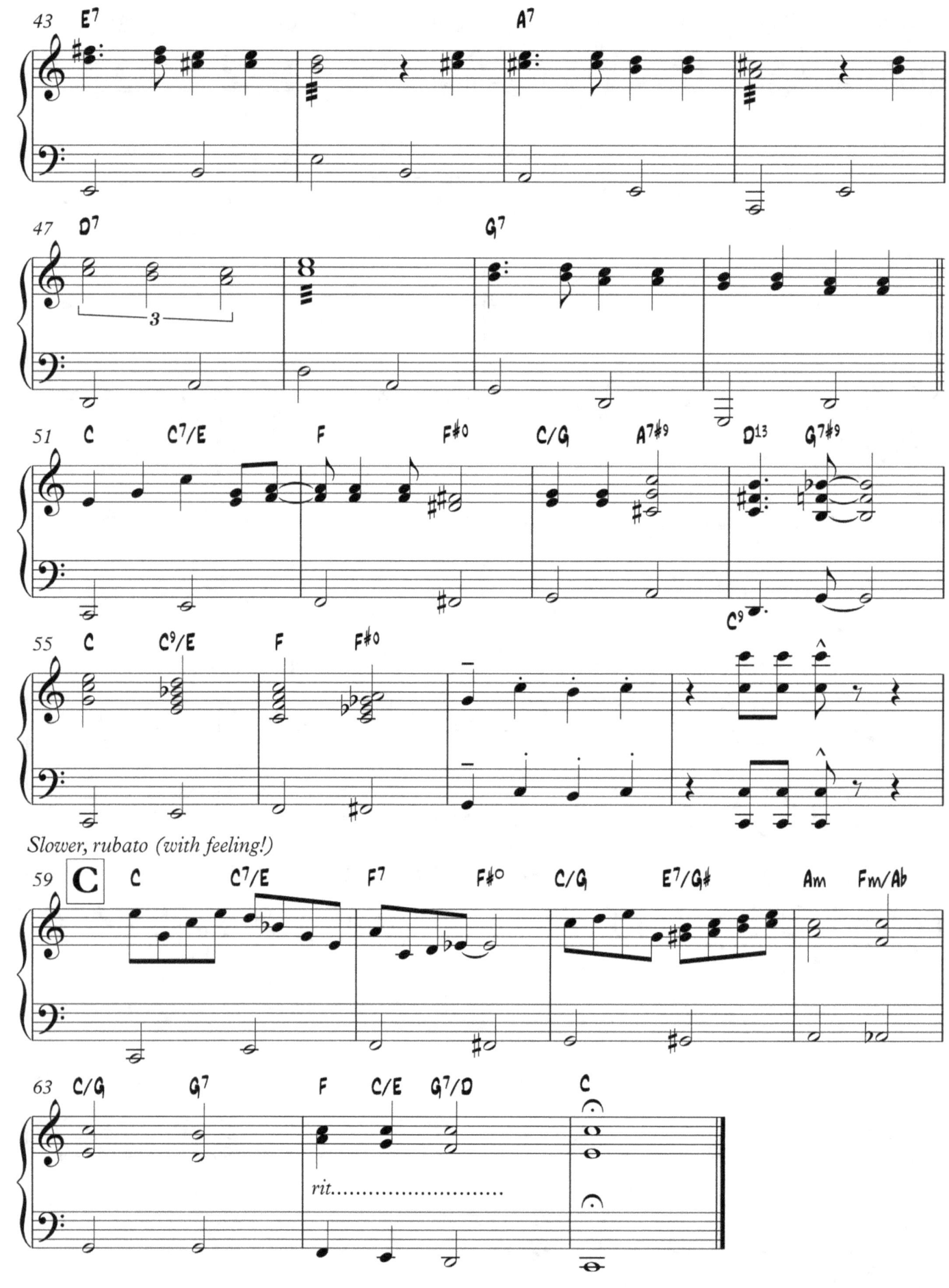

Slower, rubato (with feeling!)

rit............................

LATINESQUE II-V-I EXERCISE

This groove flows and is fun to play... if you keep the groove flowing.

As soon as you have a groove down, any groove, so you can play it without thinking, start improvising over it by creating new melodies over the left hand.

Remember, the feel of the song should not change when it's time to solo. Instead of jumping out of the song to start playing notes, try building off the song, introducing small changes that build up over time. Sometimes just changing the rhythm of the original melody can start making something happen.

Scot Ranney

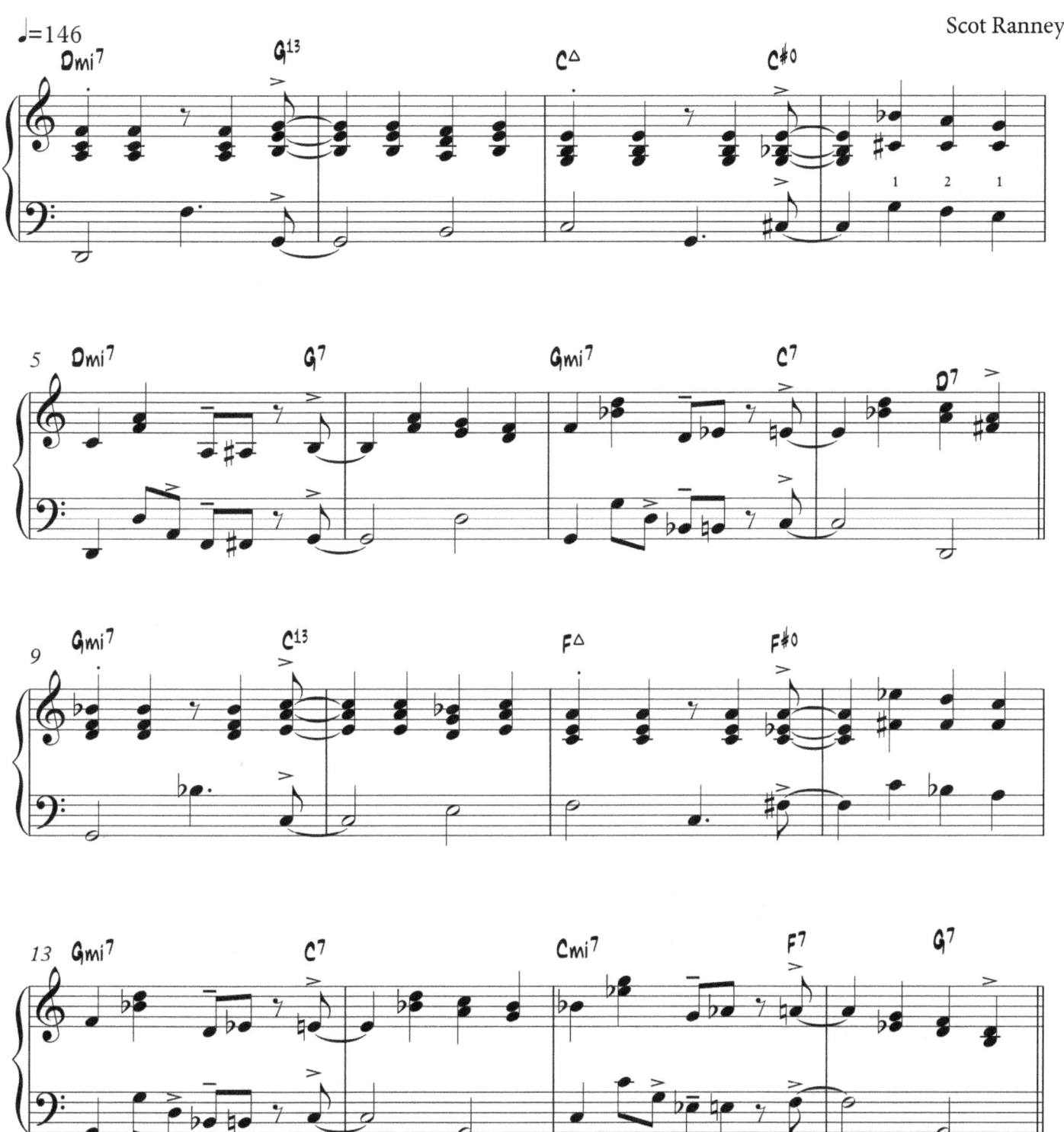

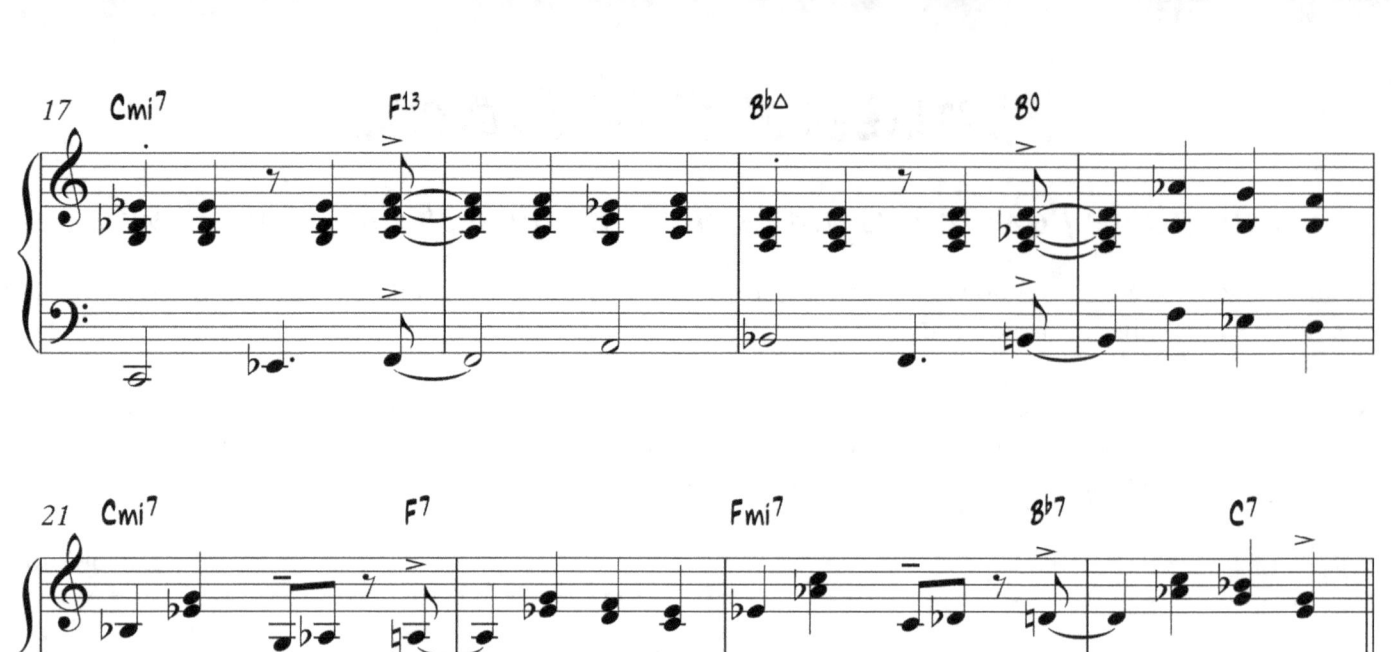

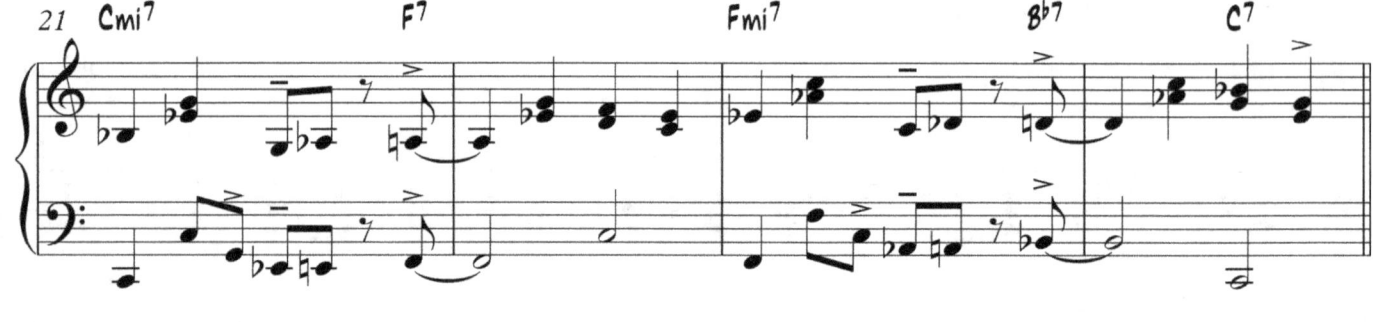

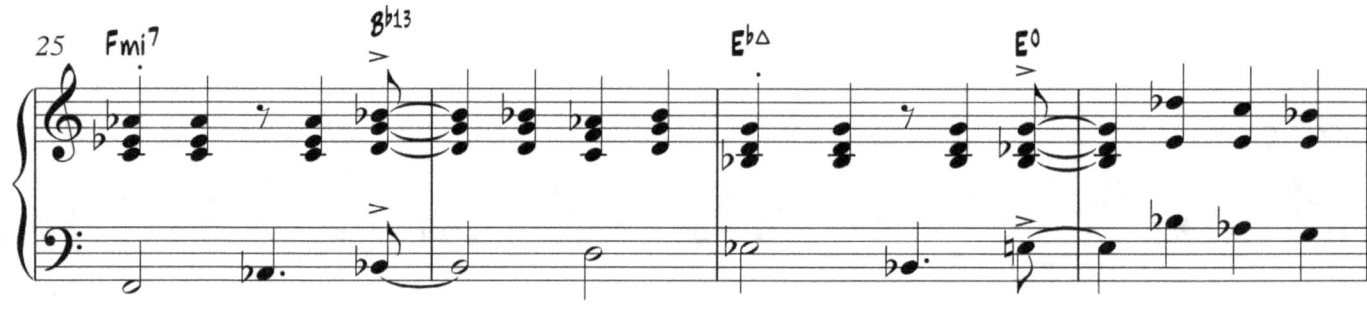

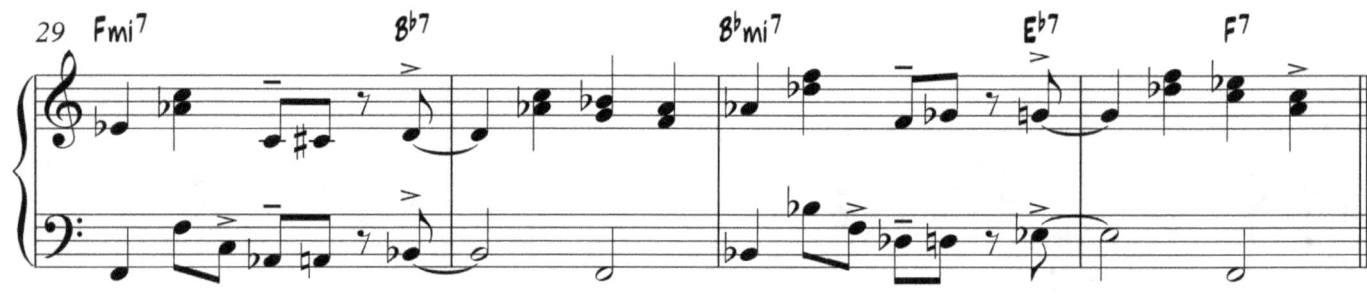

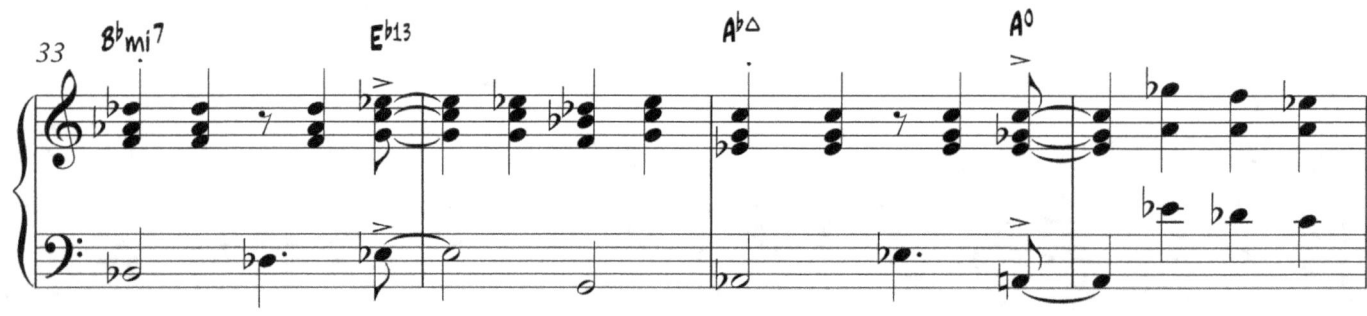

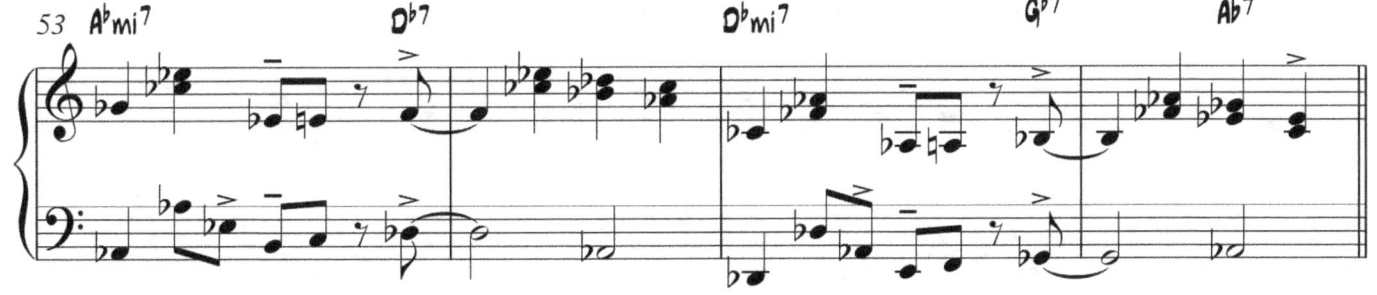

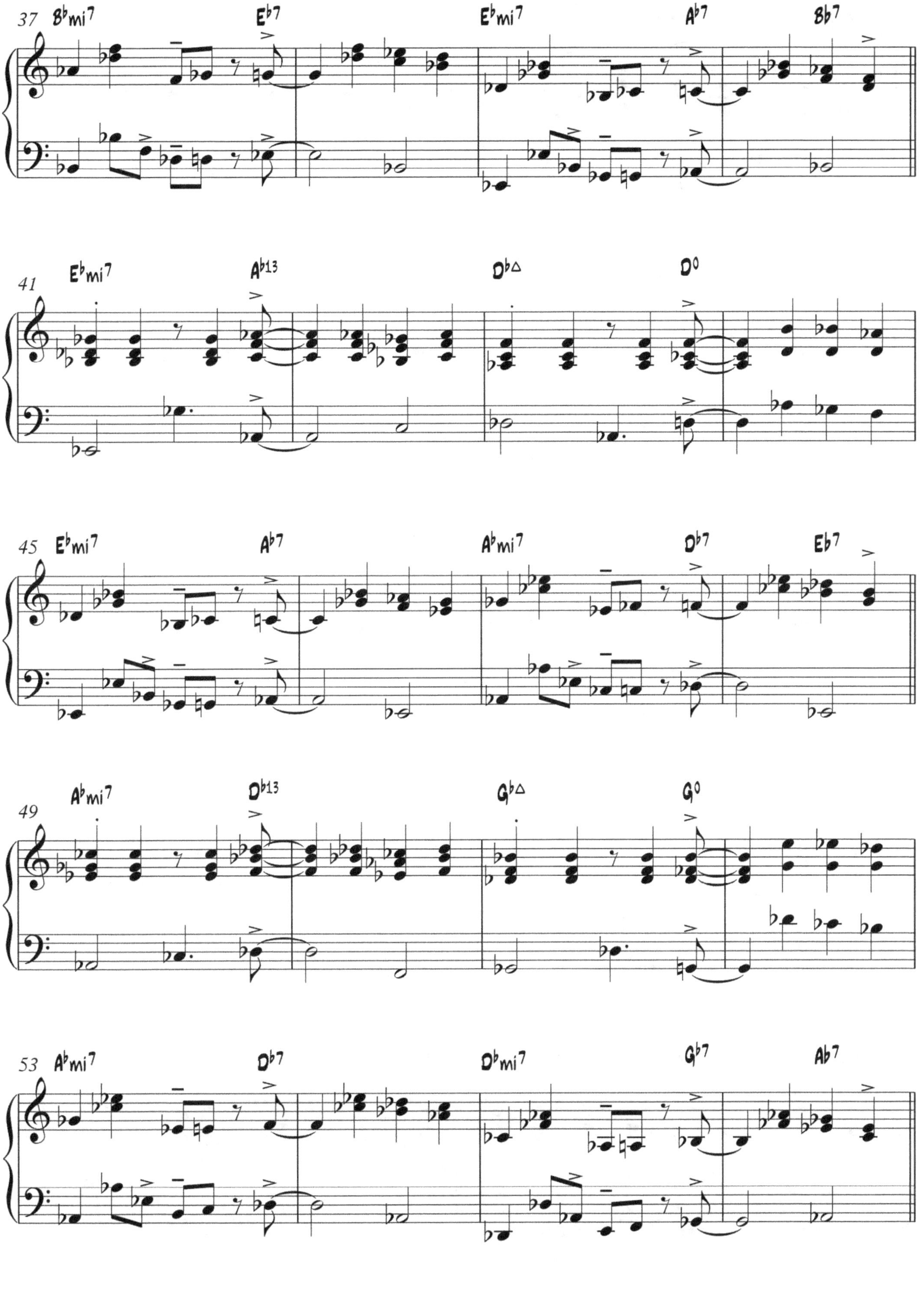

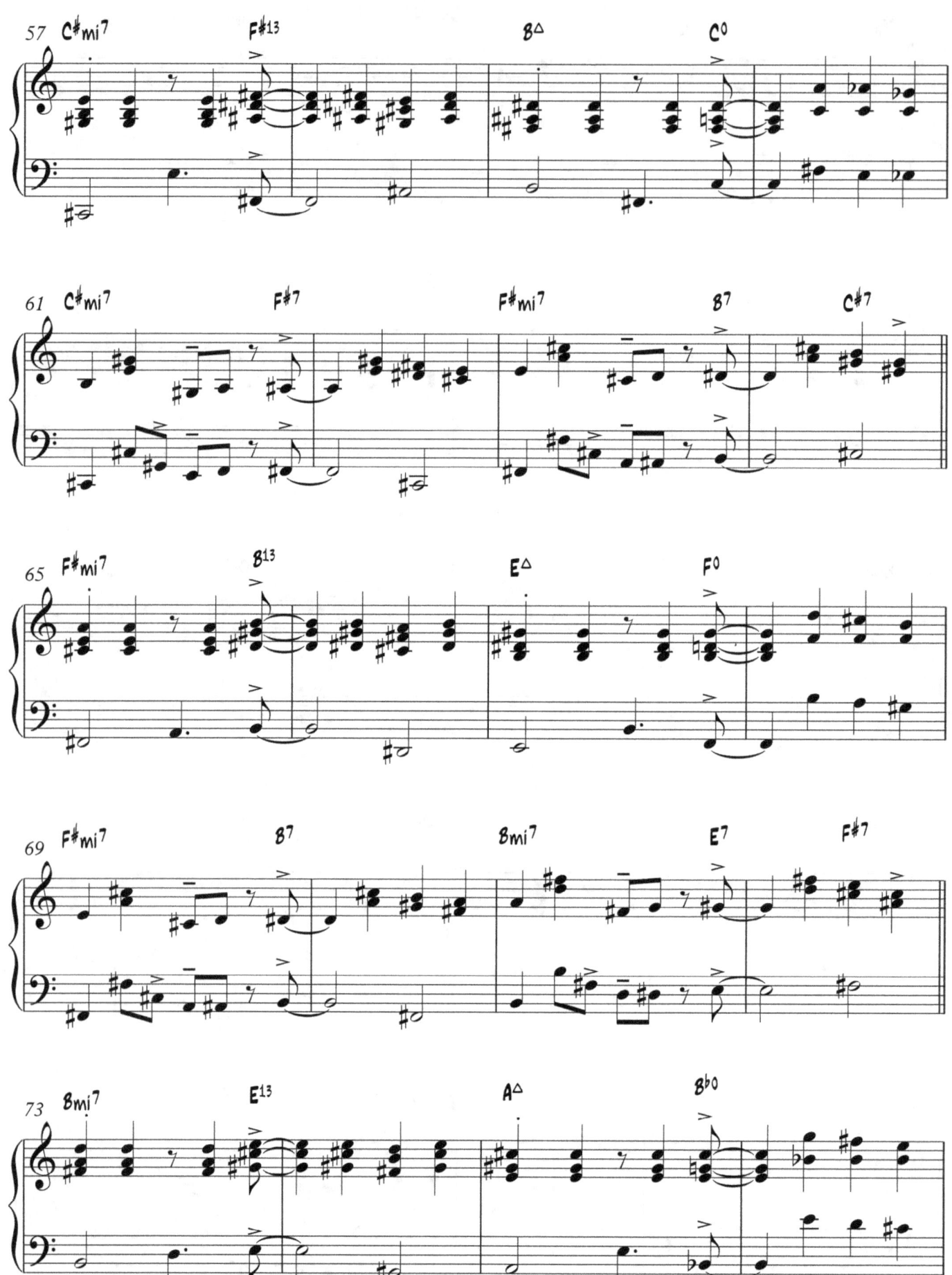

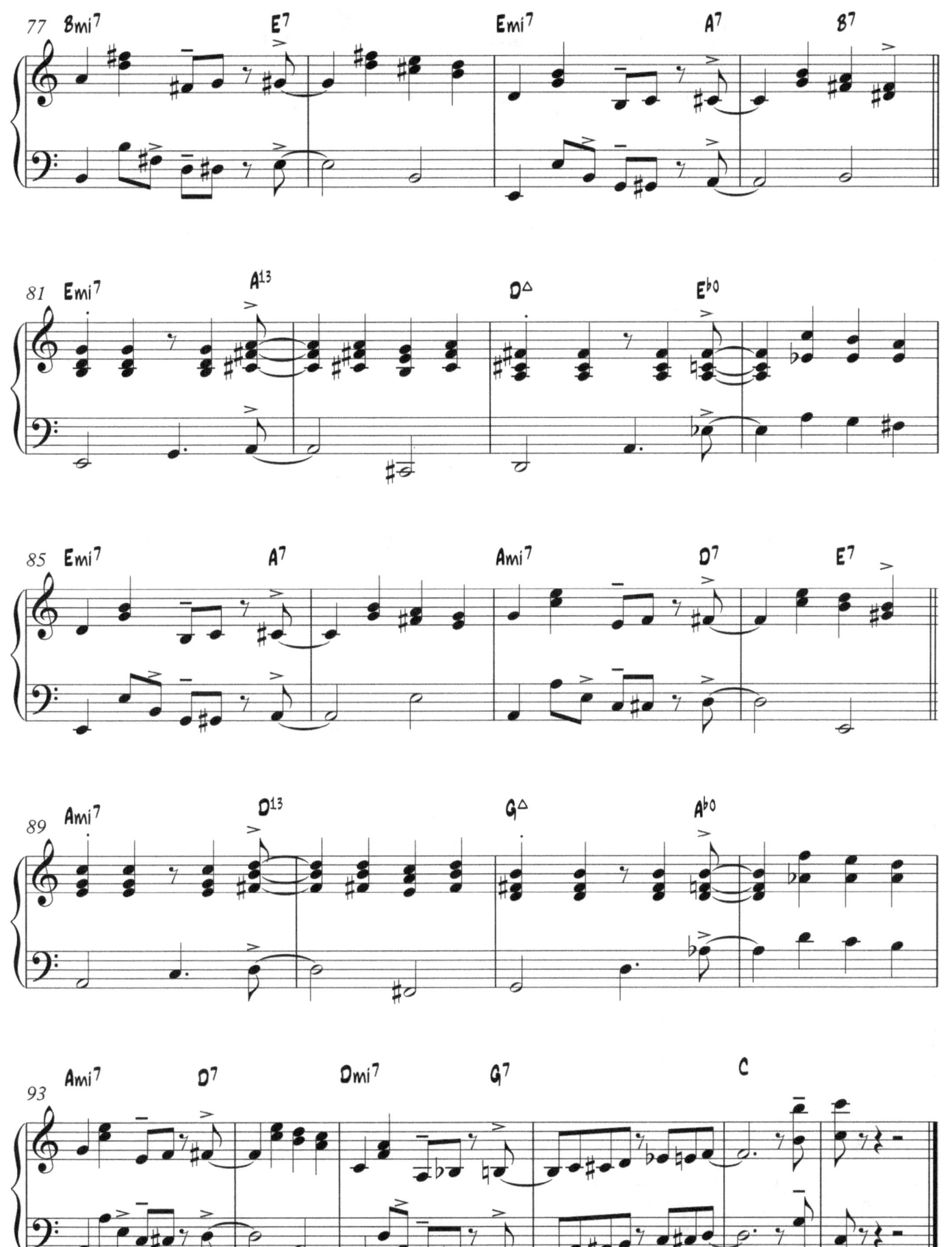

Latinesque Circle of Fifths

The most fun you've ever had just now.

This exercise helps with setting up fun rhythms to jam on and to help your fingers feel how to play this kind of material. It's a relatively short exercise but has a lot of big ideas.

You could call this a slow samba or bossa feel, maybe a basamba, but don't quote me on this (I may not know what all these latin jazz feels are called, but I know the music which is way more important!)

Play this slowly at first, metronome at 80, and make sure you get all the rhythms right. There's absolutely no reason to play this or any exercise if you don't play it accurately. **If you practice mistakes, you will learn how to play mistakes.** Being able to play something perfectly at a slow tempo makes it much easier to play it fast without mistakes.

Scot Ranney

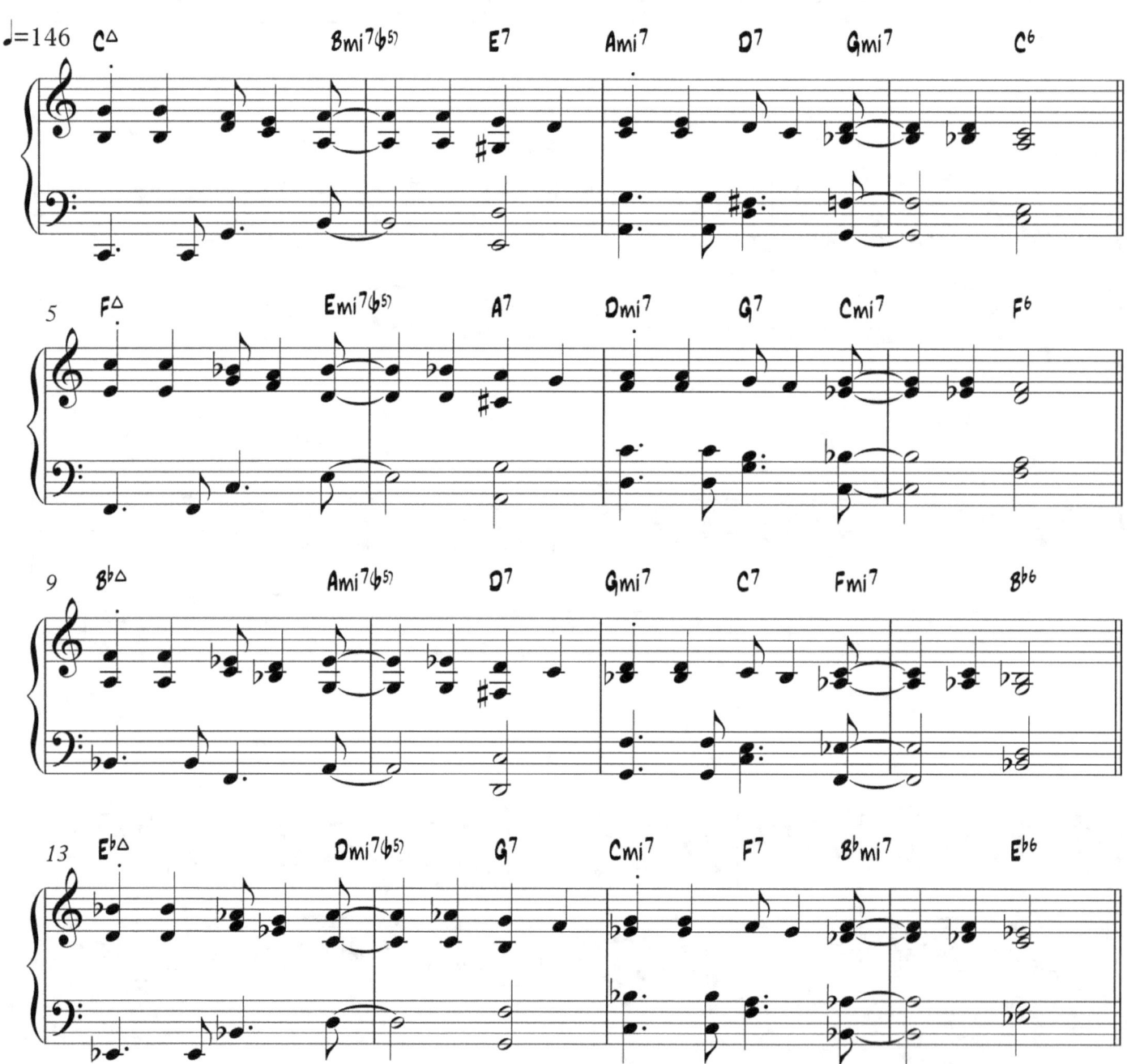

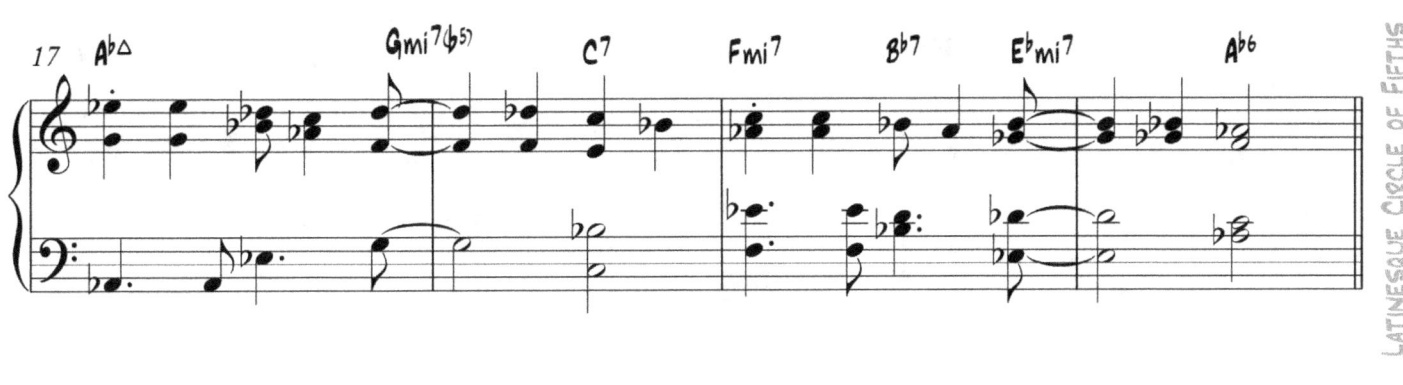

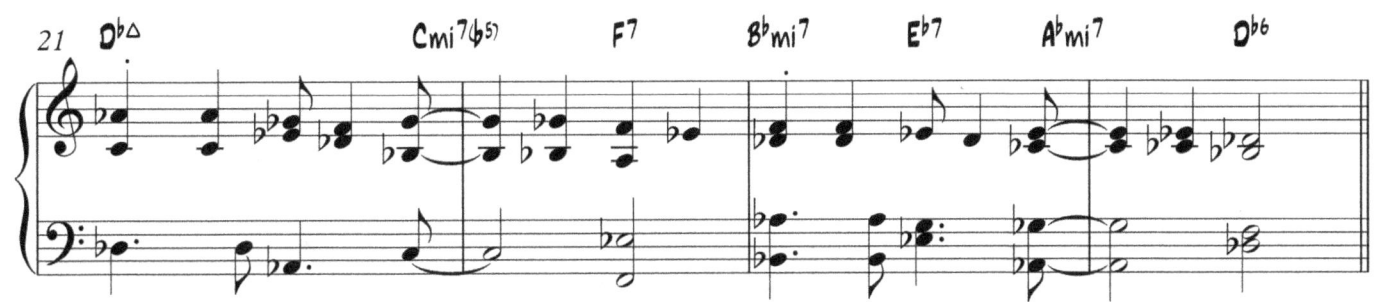

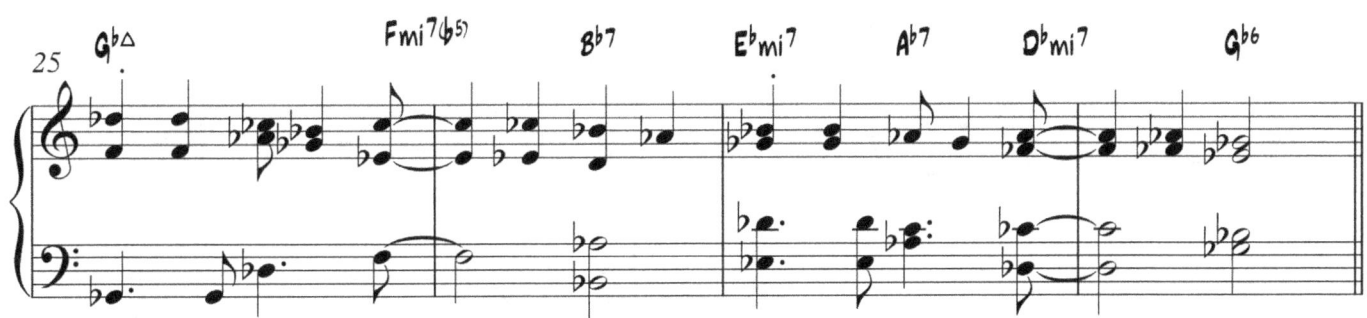

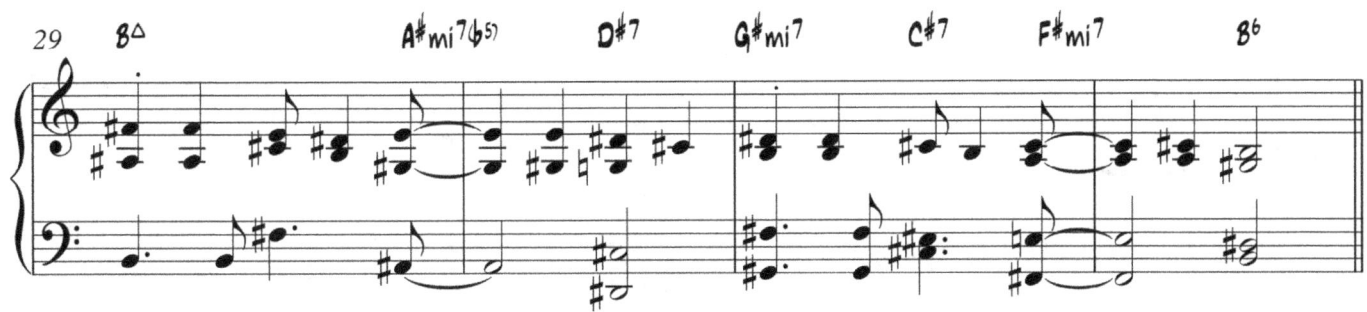

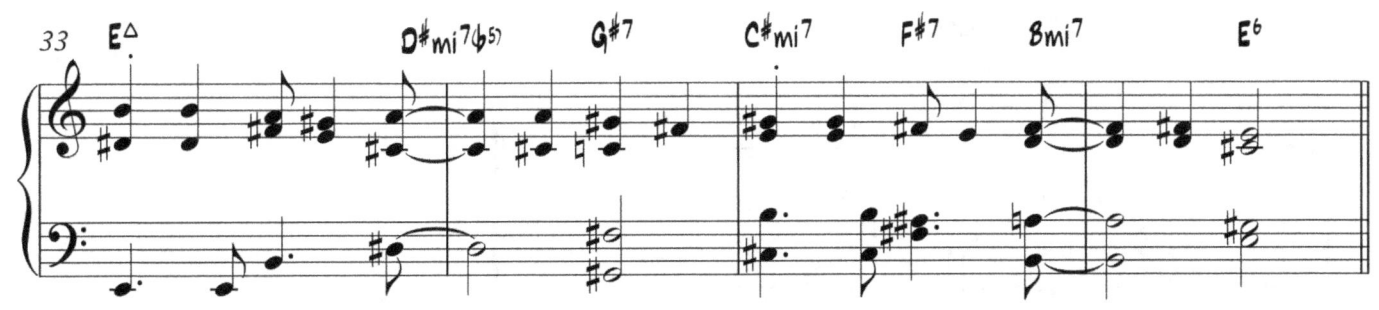

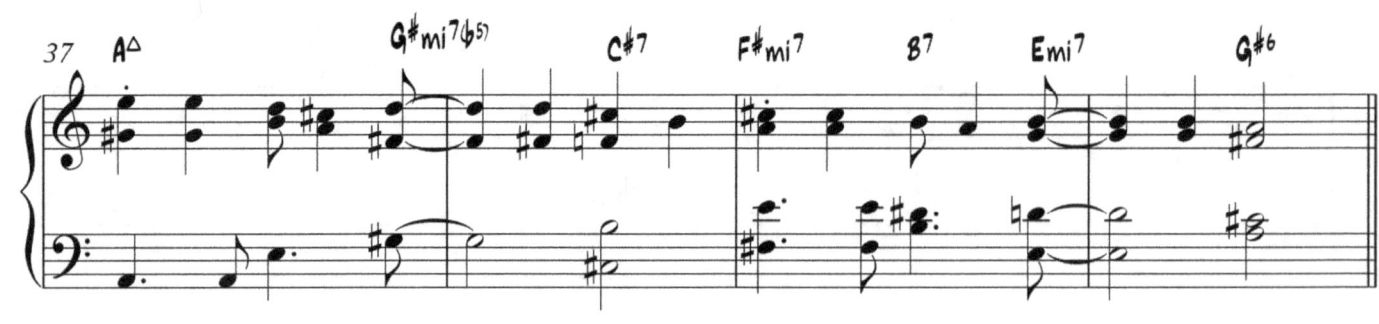

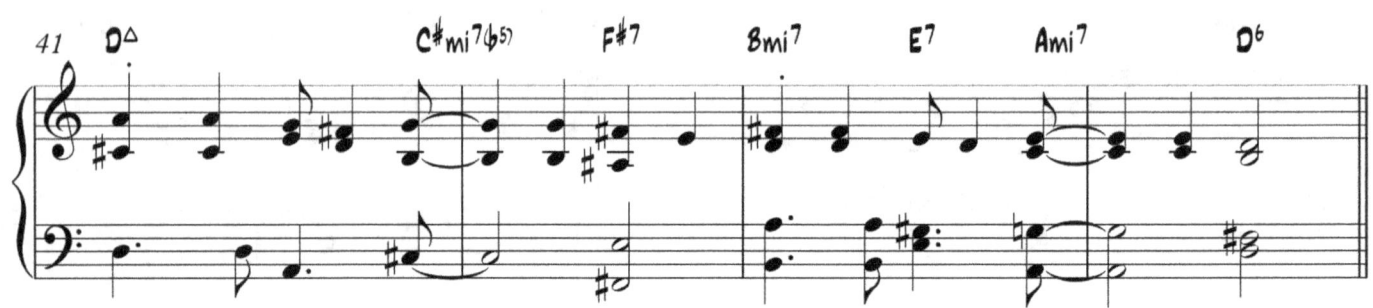

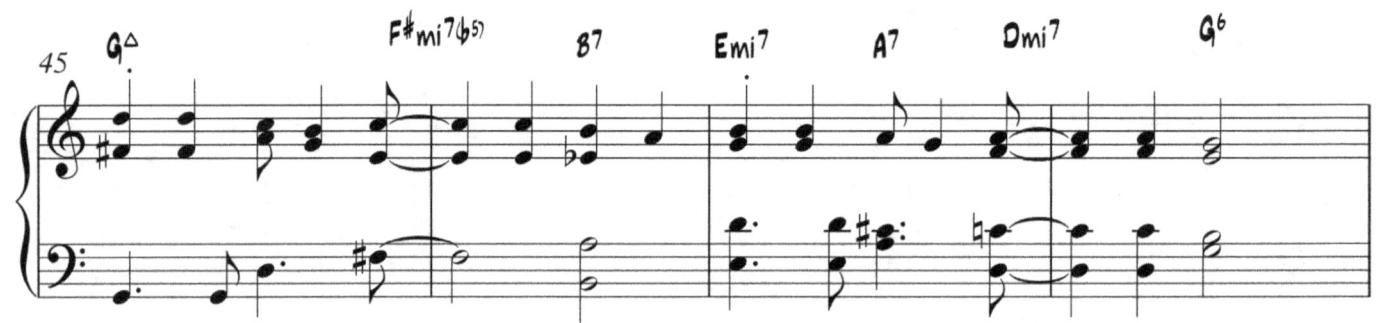

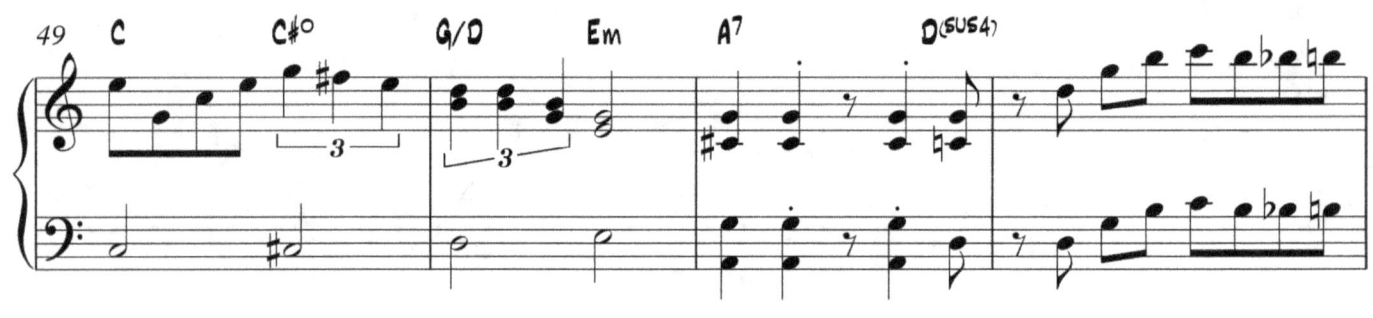

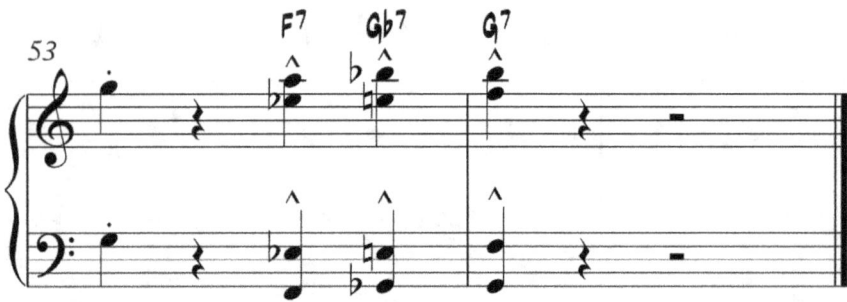

Rhythm is everything.

Your music, my music, anyone's music is defined by rhythm. People remember rhythm. People move to the rhythm. The rhythm of what you play is the foundation of your music and your connection to the audience.

If your rhythm is solid and people feel compelled to move, when you see people bobbing their heads, snapping fingers, tapping feet or dancing, you know you're doing it right. Only then will people remember things like melody or words.

The big question is, how do you get great time and play in a way that makes people want to dance?

It's easier than you think.

1. Record yourself playing and then listen to it. Many times. Use a metronome.

You know what good music sounds like. Who doesn't? It's what you like to listen to. Bad music is what you don't like to listen to.

So record your own playing as much as possible. Use your cell phone, a looper, your computer, a tape cassette recorder from 1979, it doesn't matter because all you want to do is listen to it and be as objective and honest with yourself as you can as you ask yourself these two questions:

Do you like the music enough to listen to it a lot? If not, exactly what don't you like about it?

If you don't like the music, then figure out exactly why you don't like it. Then keep that in mind when you record again. And again. And again, until you like the music. One session of this will improve your performances faster than just about anything else you can do.

2. Exaggerate!

The performer feels the music, the audience hears the music. To get the audience to feel the music the way you do, you have to exaggerate rhythmic figures and dynamics just as an actor has to exaggerate their emotions (unless it's Nicholas Cage.) What you hear at the piano only travels as far as you can reach unless you exaggerate.

3. Always hear the song.

While improvising, comping, anything- know where the melody is at all times. When you get to this point, getting lost and losing time looking for chords is a thing of the past.

You'll know when you have great time because it clicks and becomes a part of your being. You don't try to remember where you are in the music or what's coming up next anymore, you just know it.

What's that, you're still here?

Thanks for hanging out, but the book is over, time for the next thing. No, really, you've finished the book, go on, try something else.

Have you ever seen one of those movies where they throw in a surprise scene at the end of the credits? Movies like "Strange Brew" or "Ferris Bueller's Day Off" or more recently, "Deadpool's" tribute to "Ferris Bueller's Day Off". It's not quite the same with Marvel Universe movies like "Thor" and "The Avengers" because the extra scenes at the end are marketing material for the next movie.

So where was I?

Oh yeah, thanks for checking out Volume 2 of my jazz piano notebook! I hope you enjoyed going through it as much as I enjoyed making it.

Videos of the songs are available on my YouTube playlist. Sometimes it's helpful to hear the rhythms for the Latin jazz grooves:

https://www.youtube.com/user/ScotRanney/playlists

Did you enjoy this book? There are two more and others on the way:

VOLUME 1: BY SCOT RANNEY
VOLUME 2: BY SCOT RANNEY
VOLUME 3: BY TIM RICHARDS

Visit http://www.learnjazzpiano.com (LJP) to take a look.

~ Scot Ranney
January 31, 2017

AUTHORS WANTED

Do you write? Do you have an idea for a jazz piano notebook?
Contact us on LJP about becoming a jazz piano notebook author.